A CRASH COURSE IN MARKETING

A CRASH COURSE IN MARKETING

Low cost marketing strategies
that will double your sales—
not your expenses

DAVID H. "ANDY" BANGS
& ANDI AXMAN

Published by
Adams Media Corporation
57 Littlefield Street, Avon, MA 02322. U. S. A.
adamsmedia.com

ISBN: 1-58062-254-2

Printed in the United States of America.

J I H G F E D C

Library of Congress Cataloging-in-Publication Data
Bangs, David H.
A crash course in marketing: low cost marketing strategies that will double your sales, not your expenses / David H. Bangs & Andi Axman.
p. cm.
Includes index.
ISBN 1-58062-254-2
1. Marketing. I. Axman, Andi. II. Title.
HF5415 .B2838 2000
658.8'02—dc21
99-059670

This publication is designed to provide accurate and authoritative information with regard to the subject matter covered. It is sold with the understanding that the publisher is not engaged in rendering legal, accounting, or other professional advice. If legal advice or other expert assistance is required, the services of a competent professional person should be sought.

— From a *Declaration of Principles* jointly adopted by a Committee of the American Bar Association and a Committee of Publishers and Associations

Cover illustration by Don Bishop

This book is available at quantity discounts for bulk purchases.
For information, call 1-800-872-5627.

Acknowledgments

We thank our friend and editor Jere Calmes for developing the concept of this series—and for involving us in it as writers and (to a small degree) editors. Jere has a thorough understanding of the pressures facing small and growing business owners, and we're grateful to be working with him.

Cheers also go to our fellow scriveners, Bert Myer and Roger Parker, for their ideas and continuing support. The four of us meet sporadically to trade lies and complaints over food and drink. Bert and Roger make writing more fun. Thanks, guys!

Table of Contents

Section 2: *Learning about Your Market*

Section 3: *Growing Your Customer Base*

Introduction

Marketing: More Than Four P's

The tips we offer in this book are intended to augment your ongoing marketing efforts. They provide an overview of marketing, carefully edited from masses of material and culled from years of experience in our own and other businesses, as well as from chats about marketing with business owners, marketing professors, and other experts, and even from one or two of our very own mistakes. Marketing is nothing if not humbling—we still cringe at Andy's attempt to get an order for his company, Upstart Publishing, by asking a banker if he had authority to sign a check. (The banker didn't. We never could win that account!)

We have a minimalist bent: less is more, especially if it is applied. We know that too much information can be more stultifying than small amounts selectively presented. Our tips are arranged so that you can pick and choose, using them in whatever order suits your needs the best.

Whether or not you use these tips is up to you. One of our favorite quotes is by Roger Babson, the man who called the 1929 market crash and made enough money to start Babson College.

> *Experience has taught me that there is one chief reason why some people succeed and others fail. The difference is not one of knowing, but of doing. The successful man is not so superior in ability as in action. So far as success can be reduced to a formula, it consists of this: doing what you know you should do.*

Best of luck with your marketing efforts.

—ANDI & ANDY

Marketing[1] is sometimes encapsulated as the "Four P's" (product, place, price, and promotion). Although this is a useful summary, it seems to us to be too limited. So we came up with a list of our own. We call it "More Than Four P's."

1. *Product*

   This is a good place to start. You have to have something to sell. Matching your *product* (which for our purposes includes physical products, concepts, services, or solutions to problems) to a market is a key part of marketing.

   What are your deliverables? These are your products.

2. *Place*

   Conrad Hilton stated that success in hospitality businesses is due to three factors: location, location, and location. Not all businesses are as sensitive to location as hotels and restaurants, but it is a factor. You have to locate your business where your customers can easily find it—or make sure that you can deliver the goods to them in a way that they find acceptable. The delivery of product is sometimes referred to as *distribution*: How do you get the product from the factory to the consumer?

3. *Price*

   Pricing may be the most bothersome part of marketing for small business owners, who tend to either follow the market leader or simply throw up their hands and charge whatever they think might be attractive to their markets.

   However, price is a major but not the only important aspect of marketing. In most purchase decisions, price is a secondary consideration. Quality, service, availability, status, and many other factors that compose value are far more important than mere price. Otherwise we'd hire brain surgeons on the basis of low cost rather than skill.

---

[1] Marketing is defined as: 1. The act of buying or selling in a market. 2. All business activity involved in the moving of goods from the producer to the consumer, including selling, advertising, packaging, etc.

4. *Promotion*

Promotion includes all the methods we can use to reach our markets and make them aware of our products and services. These include advertisements, public relations, special promotions, and positioning. And this is just the beginning.

Now for our additional P's.

5. *Perceptions*

How your products are perceived by your market may be more important than any other single factor in marketing. You may have a superior product, but if the market doesn't recognize that it is superior, they won't buy it. Much of your market research[2] should be aimed at finding out what your market really thinks about your product. What you think doesn't matter. What your prospects think does.

6. *Positioning*

David Ogilvy claimed that in 40 years in the advertising business the most important technique he learned was positioning. How can you position your product or service in the minds of the consumers you are trying to reach? How do your goods and services differ from those of your competition?

7. *Physical distribution*

Physical distribution involves moving the product from the producer or wholesaler to the market and customer. WalMart perfected physical distribution and as a result has reinvented the retail landscape.

Though distribution is usually a concern for producers, it is increasingly important for other types of businesses. The Internet, via e-commerce, is radically changing consumer behavior—and with the ubiquitous availability of fast, reliable overnight delivery (FedEx, US Postal Service, UPS, and so on), all retailers will have to change

[2] Market research is the study of the demands or needs of consumers in relation to particular goods or services. For your sake, learn what your customers' demands and needs are.

their behaviors. By some estimates, e-commerce will account for 40 percent of all retail trade in the United States by 2004.

8. *Packaging*

   How a product is packaged is another factor in sales success. Packaging is closely related to image. Think of L'Eggs pantyhose. Better yet, think of jewelry. Tiffany's little blue boxes have a certain cachet. Or perfume: *Parfumiers* spend more on packaging than on product!

9. *Potential*

   One sure way to lose money is to plunge ahead and market a product without making sure that there is market demand for it. Don't waste efforts on duds. As a small business owner, you don't have the luxury of tossing a product onto the market without carefully thinking and researching its appeal.

10. *Professional help*

    Some beginners think they can do all the advertising and marketing themselves. Beware of false economies! There's a good reason why smart business owners invest in expert advice from professionals. They use professional help to make money. Think of professional expertise as an investment in your future profits.

11. *Planning*

    Planning is like flossing. We all know it is important and helpful and prophylactic, but it is quite often ignored in the rush of daily activity. Planning beats hopin' and wishin' for business success. It helps you look at your business and its environments from a variety of angles, helps ensure thoroughness, and may be the cheapest insurance you can buy. You need two plans: a business plan, which helps identify the broadest strategies and opportunities, and a marketing plan, which helps you achieve those profit and growth goals established in your business plan.

12. *Personnel*

Train all personnel (including yourself) who interact with the public. Lack of courtesy is the biggest single reason people stop doing business with a business, and those disgruntled customers complain to an average of 11 to 20 other people. That's powerfully negative word-of-mouth advertising. Your personnel reflect the image, reliability, and mission of your business. Train them well.

13. *Product knowledge*

If you don't know your product (or service), how can you sell it? Good presentations and demonstrations move product quickly. Even authors and artists have to be able to explain their products—why they are a good thing for the consumer, what's unusual or unique about them, how they stand out.

14. *Policies*

Policies are established to provide consistent performance. They simplify dealing with the public. Nordstrom's and L.L. Bean have capitalized on their policies of accepting returns without question or quibble. Their policies, though not without expense, probably save a lot of money in the long run by avoiding customer dissatisfaction and creating great loyalty.

Establishing policies that work is not easy. But it makes a difference.

15. *Profitability*

Profit is the sole, sane reason to be in business. You may have other worthwhile goals of a charitable or social nature, but unless you make a profit you cannot achieve those goals.

Marketing and market research are your best investments in profits. If you know who the customers are and what they want that you can provide, you are on your way to Easy Street.

16. *Prioritizing*

    Marketing is complex, with a lot of pieces that have to fit more or less seamlessly together. You set priorities to assure progress toward the goals that you establish in your business and marketing plans. Some tasks have to be done earlier than others, or are of more importance to achieving the goals. Your main job as the owner (even if you are the only employee, and part time at that) is to make sure that the important tasks are done first. That's why you set benchmarks.

    Your #1 priority: Work smarter, not harder.

17. *Preparation*

    "Be prepared" is not only the Boy Scouts' marching song—it's also great marketing advice. Marketing is too closely related to success to be left to the last moment and ad hoc solutions.

18. *Poignancy*

    What are the hot buttons your product or service presses? What do they do for your markets? Emotions are important in advertising messages since all purchasing decisions are ultimately made by individuals. A poignant ad will out-pull a dull factual ad any day of the week.

We could add more P's, but these will suffice for now.

SECTION 1:

Setting Your Marketing Goals

1

What Business Are You In?

Don't dismiss this question because it seems too obvious to answer. It isn't. For example, R.J. Reynolds forgot that its business was creating products for smokers when it introduced the smokeless Premier cigarette in 1980. Since smokeless cigarettes appeal mainly to nonsmokers, who don't buy cigarettes, lots of Reynolds' money went up in smoke as a result—$325 million to be exact. Knowing what business you're in is key to determining your target market and your competition. Not knowing what business you're in can lead to making serious marketing mistakes, losing lots of money, and possibly even to business failure.

For example, say you own a bowling alley. You're not only in business to provide pins, lanes, shoes, pizza, pinball, leagues, tournaments, trophies, and so on for people in your area who like to bowl. Your customers come to you so they can relax, unwind, get some exercise, and have a good time. Because your job is to entertain customers, not just provide them with a place to bowl, your target market isn't limited to people who bowl—it's people looking for a fun way to spend spare time, parents trying to find a place for Junior's next birthday party, busy boomers looking to get some exercise and socialize at the same time. What's more, your competition isn't just from other bowling alleys. You compete with movies, theaters, health clubs, video stores, roller-skating rinks, even restaurants and malls for customers' disposable income and for their spare time.

"We're not in the education business. We're in the transformation business. We expect everyone who participates in a program at the London Business School—whether it's for three days or two years—to be transformed by the experience," says dean John A. Quelch. The School was recently ranked by the *Financial Times* of London as the leading business school outside of the U.S. (*Fast Company*, March 1999)

Come up with a succinct definition for what business you're in. Start with the basics. Know what your business is—what you're selling to whom and why, and who your competition is.

He who knows others is wise.
He who knows himself is enlightened.

Tao-te Ching

One way to define the business you're in is by the product or service you provide. In general, the products or services most businesses sell are a lot like the products you'd find others in their field selling. A dentist sells dental-care services, a burger joint sells burgers, a record shop sells CDs and sheet music.

To stand out from the competition, your job is to find something special about your product or service and make your market aware of it. Giving your business this edge is what's referred to as "positioning," or determining your market niche.

Start by realizing that people tend to buy what they want, not what you think you offer. Your dentist just doesn't take care of teeth—he or she sells comfort by alleviating pain and anxiety, confidence by brightening smiles, convenience by having evening office hours, and peace of mind by catching little problems before they become big ones. McDonald's sells consistency and convenience—you know that you can get a burger almost anywhere on this planet that's going to taste exactly the same as the one you'd order in your hometown. Tower Records on Newbury Street in Boston offers one of the largest selections of CDs you can find anywhere.

The key question isn't necessarily "what is your product or service?" but rather "what exactly is it that you're selling?"

If a man does not keep pace with his companions,
perhaps it is because he hears a different drummer.
Let him step to the music which he hears,
however measured or far away.

HENRY DAVID THOREAU

Products and services that are not differentiated from others like them are commodities. This is how 90 percent of small businesses sell their products and services—head-to-head, with no apparent incentive for customers to buy from one rather than the other.

If you're a green grocer, what makes your flowers and vegetables different from those provided by the other shop around the corner? Since your job is to create customers, you've got to give them a reason to buy from you. Are your vegetables fresher? Are you open till 8 pm? Do you have a wide selection of flowers available that you'll also deliver? Lettuce is lettuce and a daisy is a daisy, but your challenge is to make the ones you sell most special to your customers. Find out what's important to them, and incorporate those needs and desires into your marketing strategy.

Analog Devices in Norwood, Massachusetts, has carved out a market niche for itself by providing about 800 different microchip products, each tailored to a particular application. "The lion's share of our products are proprietary and there are no second sources," said Jerald Fishman, Analog's president and chief executive in a *Boston Globe* article (February 23,

In the age of minivans, Chevrolet had a major image problem with the long-nosed Chevy Lumina, known by analysts and consumers as the "dustbuster" of the market. How could they win back consumers with their new model, the Venture? Chevy decided to knock on some doors and had anthropologists from Cultural Dynamics visit minivan owners and potential buyers at their homes to better understand them. "The cultural anthropologists discovered that the minivan was more than just a vehicle to cart people around. It was a family room on wheels," explained Dan Keller, brand manager at Chevrolet Venture/Astro. (*American Demographics*, March 1999, page 54)

Patient satisfaction soared to 96 percent—an astounding level in any industry—at Griffin Hospital in south-central Connecticut. Competition in this market is tough as it gets. Within coughing distance are seven hospitals, including the world-renowned Yale–New Haven Hospital. How does Griffin do it? In its no-holds-barred approach to fulfilling patients' wishes, Griffin includes pets among its volunteers and offers nontraditional interior design, stress-reduction sessions and personal escorts for patients. (*Inc.*, February 1999, pages 72-74)

1999). "We don't make commodity products that five or six other companies produce."

How do I work? I grope.
ALBERT EINSTEIN

Every small business owner's challenge is to make theirs a specialty product or service. So how do you take what appears to be a commodity and transform it into a specialty product or service? You start by knowing what makes your product or service different from other similar ones on the market. This is what advertising guru of the '50s Rosser Reeves called a product or service's USP or "unique selling proposition"—a competitive advantage that can be maintained and built on over time.

See how you stack up against the competition when it comes to the following: the target market you serve, price, packaging, location, quality, follow-up service, convenience, guarantees, benefits you advertise, and so on. These insights might help you position and define your business.

I am the world's worst salesman. Therefore,
I must make it easy for people to buy.
F. W. WOOLWORTH

A second way to define your business is by the market you serve. Who are your customers? Are they individuals or businesses or both? Is your market local, regional, or national? How big is it? Is it big enough so that there's a place for your business, or is it full of businesses offering a product or service like yours?

To run a successful, profitable business, you need to have detailed information on your market. Are your customers male or female? Well-heeled or middle income? College educated? Young, middle-aged, or old? Married or single? Of a particular religious or ethnic group? This information helps you determine what your target market looks like.

Once you know your target market, you can begin to estimate how many prospects are available to your business. But realize that not everyone who fits your customer profile will buy from you. You want to find those who will and make them aware of what makes your product or service stand out from those of competitors.

Competition in your market is a good sign. Lack of competition is a serious red flag. It means either you don't know what business you're in or there's no market for your product or service.

Knowledge is power.
Thomas Hobbes, Leviathan

Your business is also defined by the industry it's in. For example, Amtrak, Southwest Airlines, and Sunrise Trucking Service are all in the transportation industry, even though each has very different resources, customers, and services.

What industry is your business in, and what trends do you spot in that industry? Is the industry

When Coca-Cola introduced Surge, its entry in the heavy citrus segment of the soft-drink market, it knew Surge would appeal to males aged 12 to 24—they were already big consumers of the market's number-one citrus soda, Pepsi's Mountain Dew. (*The New York Times*, February 10, 1999)

growing? How does technology affect your industry? You want to have a clear, full picture of what your business' potential is.

To get more information on your industry, go to your library and look for trade associations in *Ayers Dictionary of Associations*. With more than 35,000 listings, it's likely that several will be good matches for your business. Many associations have magazines—write to their editors and request information on the industry they're writing about.

Who is it that can tell me who I am?
WILLIAM SHAKESPEARE, KING LEAR

One exercise to help you get a handle on how to define your business is to pretend you're sitting on a plane. You're 10 minutes away from landing, and the person next to you asks, "What business are you in?" How would you answer the question?

Your answer should include the type of business you're in (service, manufacturing, retail, hospitality, and so on), what your product or service is, who your customers are, what your goals are for the business, and how you plan to reach them. Also include the *raison d'etre* for your business—why did you start the business and what's in it for you?

What's the airplane definition for your business?

A definition is enclosing a wilderness of ideas within a wall of words.
SAMUEL BUTLER

In 1998, 25 percent of all new car purchases were researched using the Internet, according to J.D. Power & Associates. But fewer than two percent of all new cars sold were purchased using an online referral service. Still, the Web's growing popularity as an information resource is expected to morph into more e-commerce in the near future. Traditional car dealers are already in high gear—General Motors Corp has a new nationwide online buying service called GM BuyPower, which gives consumers access to all participating dealers' lots as well as independent data about competing models. Ann Blakney, national director of BuyPower, is trying to steer consumers away from Autobytel.com and AutoWeb.com, two online competitors, and maintain control over the flow of cars to the public. "We're in the car business. They're in the information business," she says. (*Business Week*, April 2, 1999)

You can condense this "airplane" definition of your business into a mission statement. Mission statements are an invaluable framework, since they sum up the long-term goals for your business and help you evaluate strategic questions as they arise.

Frances Hesselbein, former head of the Girl Scouts of America, explained the value of working out a mission statement (*Business Week,* March 26, 1990): "We kept asking ourselves very simple questions. What is our business? Who is our customer? And what does the customer consider value? We really are here for one reason: to help a girl reach her highest potential. More than any one thing, that made the difference. Because when you are clear about your mission, corporate goals and operating objectives flow from it."

Nature does nothing without purpose or uselessly.
ARISTOTLE, POLITICS

Your business' mission statement should answer these questions. Who are your most important customers? What are your products or services? What is your market area? What are your economic objectives? What values are important for your business? What is your business really good at (your USP)? What are your special concerns for your employees?

Jot down the answers to these questions, and condense them into one or two short statements. The result will be a mission statement that accurately reflects your business' purposes.

About 80 percent of Southwest Airline's business is flights shorter than 750 miles. But in late 1998 it began offering longer, non as Baltimore to Las Vegas and Austin, Texas, to Los Angeles for $99 or less. Its cost advantage is built on rapid 20-minute gate turnarounds, an efficient all-Boeing 737 fleet, and a work force that's more productive than that of its competitors. With long-haul flights a growing part of its arsenal, Southwest is seen as "a huge threat" to higher-cost competitors by a rival airline executive. (*Business Week*, February 8, 1999)

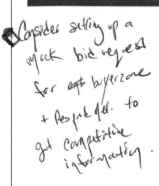

2

What Is Your Product or Service?

You have to know your product or service thoroughly, better than your customers or competitor. In particular, you should be able to answer the following questions.

- *What does the product/service do?* What results can the user expect? Another way of putting this is: What problems does the product/service help solve? People buy solutions to problems. You will sometimes have to make this clear to make a sale.
- *What are the physical characteristics of the product?* This includes such characteristics as weight, size, composition, color and malleability, freshness, origin, and a host of other things. These characteristics help to sell the product.
- *How does the product work?* If the product is technical, you better know how to use it. Demonstrations are effective only if the demonstration works. Think of presentation software: How likely are you to buy it if the salesperson fumbles and sweats and crashes his computer because he didn't take the time to rehearse?

All men by nature desire knowledge.

ARISTOTLE

> Windows 98 is Microsoft's cash cow: It has a very high market share, and is so dominant that little realistic growth in market share can be generated. Microsoft hopes to turn its Internet presence, currently a problem child, into a star, gaining share in a rapidly expanding market. Its Internet publishing ventures are dogs, yielding neither growth nor market share. Guess where Microsoft will be investing its dollars?

The Boston Consulting Group model is a helpful way to look at the products and services that you offer. While contribution to overhead and profit is important to consider when looking at your products/services' past performance, market share and market growth help decide what to do in the future.

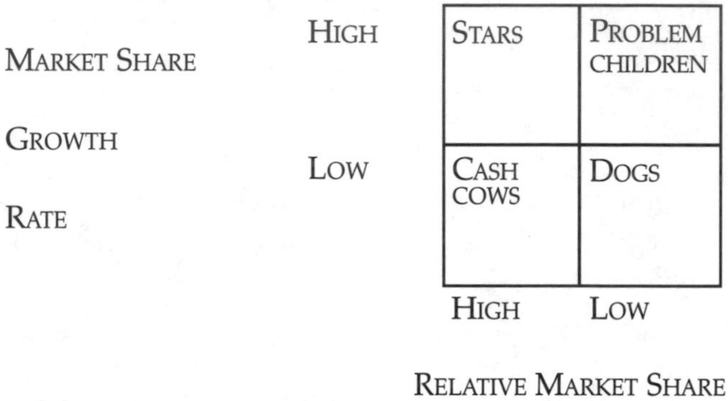

MARKET SHARE GROWTH RATE		HIGH (relative market share)	LOW (relative market share)
	HIGH	STARS	PROBLEM CHILDREN
	LOW	CASH COWS	DOGS

RELATIVE MARKET SHARE

How can this help you? Locate each of your products/services (or groups of them) by growth rate of market share and relative market share (relative to the competition). You want to focus your attention on the "stars," which yield the highest margins. "Cash cows" are those products/services that you don't have to invest much in to keep them profitable—they tend to be, well, cash cows. You want to shed the "dogs," those that have little future. The "problem children" need to be very carefully examined since they can become "stars" or "dogs" in a relatively short time.

Hitch your wagon to a star.

RALPH WALDO EMERSON

The features (sometimes called characteristics) of your product/service are an important piece of the marketing puzzle. Try making a laundry list of the product features, which will probably include some benefits. That's good; the more benefits the better. Suppose you are selling wallpaper. The features of the various wallpapers might include the material they are made of, size and weight, the colors of the design, the patterns and textures, the ruggedness or delicacy of the paper, the glossiness or light absorbing qualities. Maybe this kind of wallpaper is easy to clean (a benefit?). Maybe a color is unique, or a special backing is provided to cover gaps in the wallboard.

Now make your list. In one column put all the features, one per line. In the next column, write down what benefits you think might be conveyed by the feature. Ask customers, prospects, suppliers, and friends to play this game. It can be fun. It will certainly be informative. Leave this process open-ended: You will not capture all the relevant ideas in your first pass, nor in the next one.

It is the province of knowledge to speak, and it is the privilege of wisdom to listen.

OLIVER WENDELL HOLMES, SR.

Another way to understand your product/service is in terms of the customer needs it fulfills. These needs fall into two broad categories: unmet needs (these call for some educational effort on your part) and perceived needs. It is easy to sell aspirin to someone with

Part of John Kirkpatrick's California citrus farm is tied to some of the most devout Jewish communities in America. Kirkpatrick is said to be the only large-scale U.S. producer of the *esrog*, known in English as the citron. The bumpy, yellow fruit is used to celebrate the Jewish holiday of Sukkot, which commemorates the autumn harvest, and retails for $50 or more apiece—about 200 times the price of a lemon. The *esrog* operation has become a significant part of Kirkpatrick's family business—and more. The church-going Presbyterian now speaks some Yiddish and is so steeped in certain aspects of Jewish law that he jokingly refers to himself as "Rabbi Kirkpatrick." (*The Wall Street Journal*, April 27, 1999, A-1)

Coca-Cola's national accounts program has long been noted as a leader in integrating sales, marketing and any other group that might touch the customer. Coke devotes employees from sales, marketing, finance, operations and support. "They'll converge on a market, and research the people, the culture, the sociology and debrief each other," says Cheryl Stallworth-Hooper, a former Coke employee who's now a marketing consultant. "Because of that, there's a great expanse of knowledge that they gain." (*Sales and Marketing Management*, April 1999, page 32)

a headache. It's somewhat more difficult to sell life insurance to a 22-year-old bachelor. In the first case, the need is present, compelling, and clearly perceived. Slam dunk. In the second case, the need is less than apparent, perhaps not perceived as a need even after extensive educational efforts by the sales agent. This doesn't mean that there is no need, just that it is not acute enough to be a spur to action.

If you can describe your product or service in terms that reveal a need that your customer can identify as important, your chances of making a sale go way up. How can you do this?

You can wing it. This is why salespeople sometimes babble and stutter. They haven't thought through the use of the product from the customer's point of view, but only from their own.

Knowledge is of two kinds. We know a subject ourselves, or we know where we can find information upon it.

SAMUEL JOHNSON

Or you can rehearse ahead of time. This is similar to listing all the relevant features of the product, then looking for the benefits that those features convey or could be made to convey to the customer. Make a list of all possible needs that the product or service might satisfy. Again, this is an open-ended list, one that will be greatly improved by having your friends, customers, suppliers, and so on help you generate. None of us are wise enough to recognize all the needs our products/services satisfy or help satisfy.

Once you have the list, look for *major* needs that might be satisfied. These will vary from one product or service to another, but will have family resemblances. Some may be health needs: nutrition, sanitation, prevention. Some may be social needs: status, affiliation or membership, recognition. Some may be financial needs: income, security, return. There are other sets of needs that you can come up with.

This is by no means a simple exercise, but working through it will help you understand your products' values from your prospects' point of view. That is worth all the effort.

The world is an oyster but you don't crack it open on a mattress.

ARTHUR MILLER

Perceived benefits are more useful to you than any possible feature because perceived benefits are what people buy. Or why they buy. A benefit that is not perceived is hardly an impetus to purchase. You have to understand your product in terms of the perceived benefits it provides.

Part of the perceived benefit equation is obvious: People won't buy junk (unless they think it a great bargain, which is a perceived benefit of another sort). A certain level of quality and availability and ease of purchase is expected. Beyond this base level, though, perceptions can be affected through education, advertising, demonstrations, testimonials, and all the other promotional efforts that are available.

The Brick Store in Bath, New Hampshire, has found success by linking the past with modern marketing. Although there's a supermarket and a WalMart five miles up the road, The Brick Store thrives by catering to both locals and tourists. "Charm sells," says state agricultural commissioner Steve Taylor, a New Hampshire native who owns a farm farther south. (*The Concord Monitor*, April 12, 1999, B-2)

Phillips Treleven, the owner of Thorndike Press (a large print publisher), ran a survey which showed that librarians (his largest market) viewed ease of ordering to be more important than range of titles. He also found that the traditional large print publishers were concentrating on Bibles, health books, and similar titles, while the readers (the end users) were clamoring for thrillers, romances, fiction, cookbooks, and all the other books that normally sighted people read. And were complaining to their librarians about the dearth of entertaining reading. So he benefited twice: He found one of the librarians' hot buttons and found a huge new market.

WYSIWYG (What you see is what you get).
COMPUTER TERMINOLOGY

Think of your products or services as a bundle of features and benefits. There aren't any pure products, and very few services don't involve some material medium to convey value. If you can think of your product or service in terms of what the customer gets—the bundle of features and benefits—you will be successful.

Your "reasons to buy" from McDonald's go far beyond the product. McDonald's definition of what they provide is QSC: Quality, Service, and Cleanliness. Note that they don't say "we sell hamburgers and fries and cookies and shakes and..." They found that their customers valued the consistent quality of product and service to be found in McDonald's the world over. But the greatest value of all is cleanliness. A McDonald's motto is "If you have time to lean you have time to clean." You know that McDonald's will have clean floors, spotless windows and tables, immaculate bathrooms. Ask any mother traveling with children why she stops at Mickey D's. Hint: It isn't the food. McDonald's has brilliantly bundled values with their products. Worried about conservation? Plenty of customers were, so McDonald's changed their packaging. Worried about fat content? OK. They modified their menu and reviewed ways to lower cholesterol in their meals.

Naming products is a special art. The right name can make it easier for your market to identify your product as something they want. The wrong name can have unexpected consequences. This is most noticeable in selling into foreign markets.

Chevrolet found that their Nova line flopped in Spanish-language markets. "Nova" means "doesn't go" in Spanish—hardly an inducement to buy a car. In one Chinese dialect, Coca-Cola translated as "Bite the wax tadpole." What were they thinking?

A good name is rather to be chosen than great riches.
PROVERBS, 22:1

It can be hard to imagine that what you sell is a product, especially if you primarily are selling a service. We call these "odd products."

Consultants sell solutions, disguised as neatly typed reports with graphics, charts, to-do lists, software, videos, or other visual representation of the solution. The product (physical manifestation) is part of the service. The benefits that provide value may be peace of mind, supporting data for a previously made solution, confirmation of a hunch. Even the benefits have to be made somewhat tangible. A verbal report is vaguely unsatisfying to the customer.

If you have difficulty viewing your service as a product, think of the person who will be buying it. How can you provide something that he or she can touch, feel, see that makes your service tangible?

Protection is not a principle, but an expedient.
BENJAMIN DISRAELI

Another helpful product question to raise is "Who uses it?" This should be separated from another valuable question "Who pays for it?"

We used to write newsletters to help major banks' trust and commercial banking departments position themselves as more user-friendly than the next bank, concerned with Community Reinvestment Act compliance and a colleague of sorts for the customer base. To sell this editorial service, we created hero kits for mild-mannered, midlevel bankers. This included collateral material to help them present our service to their superiors in such a way that if the program succeeded the boss would recognize them as heroes, but if the program failed they could blame us, thus not losing face. Thus an important part of our product was job protection for our bank contacts.

Look at your products and product line, and make sure to know who uses it—and who pays for it.

Where money talks, there are few interruptions.
HERBERT V. PROCHNOW

Product life cycles are a good way to look at your product's potential. Products go through a predictable sequence of four stages: introduction, growth, maturity, and decline. The stages have a powerful impact on how to market the product. Each stage has defining characteristics.

- *Introduction.* When products are new, profits are low because you have to educate the market. There may be no direct competitors, which allows higher prices, but since few people are "early adopters" sales will be low.
- *Growth.* As market awareness grows, competitors enter. Sales rise quickly, and price competition is unlikely.
- *Maturity.* At this point, there will be lots of competitors, and price competition will become intense. Sales flatten as substitute products siphon off some customers. Profits tend to be flat or declining. There may be some consolidation of competitors.
- *Decline.* The product is on its way out, becoming obsolete as the market turns its attention to newer products. Profits decline.

When one door shuts, another opens.

ANON

Some marketing problems stem from flawed supplier relations. Your customers want and expect your products to be available when they want them, at the level of quality they expect from that product. If you rely on suppliers for product, make sure that they can continue to supply you if your orders increase—and that they can maintain the level of quality that made their products desirable in the first place.

With moderate effort, you can create a symbiotic relation with your key suppliers. Maybe you bind them to you by paying them promptly, or order during their slow production period, or arrange to take delivery at their convenience rather than at your own. Use you wits: Your ingenuity can make a difference. Steer customers to them, help them with a new technology, introduce them to a friendly banker or financier, or help them keep on top of their markets. The returns to you will be great: steady supply, preferred treatment if demand goes through the roof, maybe better prices.

Remember that business is a two-way street. Your suppliers are as much a key to your success as you are to theirs.

Consider the plight of the publishers of *My Weekly Reader*. This innocuous publication had a huge readership, almost entirely composed of children in grade school. Under a new publisher, the wheels came off the marketing wagon. Looking at the product, which was clearly aimed at helping children learn to read and understand something about the world around them, they decided to make it even more appealing to the children than before. They succeeded. Unfortunately, it turned out that the teachers no longer liked the product, and since they are the ones who pay for it (or arrange for payment) sales plummeted.

It is possible to make money with declining products. Underwood, the maker of deviled ham, took advantage of a market gap for tinned meats when most of the major competitors bailed out of a shrinking market. A small business such as Underwood can revive a market niche that is too small for the giants.

You can learn as much from negative examples as from positive instructions. There are five common product-related errors.

First is failure to appreciate that products are service driven. Every business is a service business—there are no exceptions. Your products can be wonderful and your knowledge of them exhaustive, but unless your market has access to them at a price they are willing to pay, you'll be stuck with aging inventory.

Second is ignorance of how your market wants your products to be made available. There is a wonderful song in *Ain't Misbehavin'* called "Find Out What They Like," which goes on "and how they like it, and give it to them just that way." Great advice. That's what market-driven companies like Coca-Cola, McDonald's, and WalMart do. Product-driven companies fail because the market doesn't care that you have made the proverbial better mouse trap unless it is what they like. A market-driven approach is much more effective and profitable.

Loyalty is the Tory's secret weapon.
LORD KILMUIR (SIR DAVID MAXWELL FYFE)

Third is that no amount of armchair research will help you know what products your market really wants. Secondary information from magazines, newsletters, and similar written sources is useful. But nothing beats getting out there and talking directly with your customers. Get in their faces. Listen to them. Ask them what they like and how they like it.

People like to be asked for their opinions. You can use your judgment to evaluate their responses (some will try to please you, others won't understand the question, yet others will ramble on and on). Their direct responses are invaluable to you.

Fourth, you never, never "own the customer" because you are the sole supplier. Complacency breeds commercial disaster. We worked with a chain of banks in a rural area that claimed that they had no need of promotion because they were the only show in town. When banking deregulation flattened them, they were bewildered: Why would their long-term customers leave them for a newcomer? Maybe better hours, rates, and services made a difference after all.

Finally, product perfection prevents profitability. Picture a binding machine for long magazine runs. It stands eight feet tall and 150 feet long, a gorgeous Rube Goldberg contraption that collates, binds, staples, folds, trims, and clatters merrily along. Now look at its control panel. Does it matter if it is the size of a pack of cards or a breadboard? One of our former clients was in this industry and failed to get their product delivered on time because they wanted to miniaturize the control panel. Their competition went ahead with a breadboard (not beautiful but effective) and put them under.

I wish to preach, not the doctrine of ignoble ease, but the doctrine of the strenuous life.

THEODORE ROOSEVELT

Sparks Department Store in Malden, Massachusetts, is one of the few surviving retail stores that once dominated the Main Streets of America. Its secret of success? Sparks is all about fashion at low prices. And as an independent, it's nimble. If a customer wants a particular ladies slack and they're out of her size, within minutes the salesperson is on the phone with the manufacturer placing an order. Salespeople treat each customer personally, and engender the customer loyalty critical for a small retailer. (*Business Week*, "A Mom-and-Pop Store Defies the Odds," April 12, 1999)

3

What Are Your Marketing Goals?

The first step in the market-planning process involves setting goals. Not only do goals provide direction—they also give you an idea of what success will look like and help you achieve it by providing a focus for your attention.

The goals you set should strike a balance between what's actually achievable and what's really pie in the sky. Although it's important to set your sights high, you need to be realistic about your resources, your time frame, your market, and trends in your industry. Remember that there will always be circumstances and other factors beyond your control.

Goals are not meant to be engraved in stone. As your business grows and your life circumstances change, and as you gain more experience managing your business, you will fine-tune and revise your goals.

A man's reach should exceed his grasp,
Or what's a heaven for?
ROBERT BROWNING, "ANDREA DEL SARTO"

There are two types of goals every business owner needs to set: personal goals and business goals. Personal goals come first because you don't want to commit your business to a strategy that clashes with your lifestyle or

Charles Brewer, founder of MindSpring, an Internet service provider in Atlanta, left a career in the software industry after becoming frustrated with corporate cultures that stifled talent and innovation. Eager to launch a business that embodied humble and humane ideals, he crafted nine statements of "core values and principles," including homilies such as "We insist on giving our best effort in everything we undertake." He prints those rules on the back of all MindSpring business cards. (*The Wall Street Journal*, March 3, 1999, B-1)

prevents you from realizing your dreams. Personal goals should also reflect personal values.

For example, do you see yourself working till you drop, or will you retire at age 55? Do you envision your company growing to 50 or more employees, or do you see yourself remaining a lone eagle? Will you sell the business in a few years and move on to something else? Will your business position you as an innovator in your field? Or is your business an outgrowth of a hobby, something you do just for fun? Is there a cause you're passionate about and want reflected in your business, such as environmental conservation or helping people with disabilities? Each of these personal goals has been cited by small business owners, and each has profound marketing implications.

What are your personal goals for the next year? Three years? Five? Jot them down, and refer to them as you work through the market-planning process.

Setting business goals comes next. Do you foresee growing the business into one of the Inc. 500? Or would you rather keep the business small and home-based? Do you see your business expanding into other product lines? Do you see an opportunity to franchise your business down the road? Will you sell the business once it reaches a certain level or growth? Or do you plan to pass the business on to your kids? Or establish an ESOP (Employee Stock Ownership Plan) for your employees?

These goals also have a profound impact on your market-planning efforts.

What are your business goals for the next year? Three years? Five? Write these down, too.

Long-range planning does not deal with future decisions, but with the future of present decisions.
PETER F. DRUCKER

For help setting your marketing goals, return to your mission statement (see Chapter 1, page 9 for a review). Your marketing goals are a logical outgrowth from your mission statement and advance the reasons you're in business in the first place.

Your marketing goals create the framework for your market plan—a written document that helps you manage the process of creating customers for your product or service over a one-year period. Your market plan outlines the action steps necessary to making the plan work.

Action steps include specific, measurable results you want to achieve in your business. They could be the number of new customers or the percentage of increase in sales you want to have by the end of the year, introducing the Web site you're developing, the local advertising you'll do in the coming year, and so on. Your goals need deadlines, as well as a point person responsible for achieving them.

Your market plan should also include image goals. They describe how you want to be perceived by your market. Do you want to be better known? The industry leader? Do you want to change the way you're known? If your business is just getting off the ground, if it's suffering from an outdated image, or if it has experienced significant growth, image goals will be a big part of your marketing plan.

"Visibility for women business owners, women in management and other professions" is Vicki Donlan's goal for *Women's Business*, a monthly business-to-business newspaper published in Boston. As the only publication in its area focusing on this business segment, *Women's Business* features women with different skills and decision-making roles discussing their businesses and their work—not life-style issues. (*The Boston Sunday Globe*, March 14, 1999, G-4)

Act quickly, think slowly.

GREEK PROVERB

Goals for sales and profits need to be precise. When you forecast sales, use a best-case/most-likely-case/worst-case approach. This winds up being a lot more accurate than guessing.

In addition, a service-by-service or product-by-product approach produces a much more accurate forecast than lumping all of your sales together without differentiating them.

For each product or service, estimate what sales would be if everything went perfectly. Then estimate what they'd be if everything went wrong. Since neither of these scenarios is likely, an in-between figure is more realistic. Don't use an average of best-case and worst-case figures here. Instead, make your best educated guess as to what's most likely to happen with sales over the next year.

Profit goals are more difficult to establish. If you know what profit you traditionally make as a percentage of sales, use the sales forecast and add a bit. You don't want to underestimate profits, and your business will (you hope!) become more profitable as sales increase.

Setting sales and profit goals makes your broad marketing objectives more precise, which helps you set benchmarks for measuring progress toward your goals.

The only real gauge of success we have is profit—honest profit.

REX BEACH

Once you have a good idea of what your marketing goals are, you can begin working on ways to reach them. These strategies are the essence of your marketing plan.

Writing a marketing plan is easy because you don't write it until you've done 95 percent of the work. The hardest part of market planning is performing a careful examination of your business, including product and service analysis, analyses of your markets and your position in them, and analysis of the strengths and weaknesses of your business.

A SWOT analysis is one way to make wise choices in choosing marketing strategies for your business. SWOT stands for strengths, weaknesses, opportunities, and threats. By capitalizing upon your strengths and shoring up your weaknesses, you maximize your ability to take advantage of opportunities and minimize threats.

SWOT analysis begins by looking at internal strengths and weaknesses in these areas: profitability, sales and marketing, quality, customer service, productivity, financial resources, financial management, operations, and distribution. Make sure to involve your employees in this process. Not only can they provide valuable feedback, but working through this process with them gives you an opportunity to reinforce their importance to your company.

Next, look at the external environments where your business operates. The areas you want to cover include current customers, prospects, competition, technology, political climate, government and other regulatory bodies, legal environment, and economic environment. To understand how technology can

How large a market needs to be is always a relative question. Budweiser needs to sell an awful lot of suds to many millions of people, because of its relationships with more than 900 wholesalers and a commitment to spending about $100 million a year to advertise its brand. The 700 or so microbreweries in the U.S. have revenues much less than those at the huge breweries, but the margins must be enticing. There were only 75 microbreweries in the country in 1990. (Robert M. McMath, *What Were They Thinking?* New York: Times Books, 1998, page 15)

forever change what we do and how we do it, think of how desktop publishing revolutionized the publishing, typesetting, and printing industries.

Pick no more than five strengths and opportunities to focus on, and no more than five weaknesses and threats to concern yourself with. Choose them carefully. By limiting your choices, you'll be able to focus your attention on areas with the biggest rewards.

Opportunities are usually disguised as hard work, so most people don't recognize them.
Ann Landers

Knowing what strengths you'll build on and which weaknesses you'll bolster will help you pinpoint your marketing strategies. Do you have a specialty or area of expertise worth promoting? Is the market for your goods or services growing? Are you undercapitalized? Is competition rife in your market?

What you're aiming for in this process is to figure out what to focus on, discover which small market niches to dominate, and determine how to please customers more than your competitors can.

One of the biggest impediments for achieving your marketing goals is the competition. Every business has it. You're not the only business looking to your target markets for your next sale.

Start assessing your business' competitive environment by identifying your immediate competitors. Who are they? What do they do better than you? What do you do better than your competitors? Are they investing in new products, services, or tech-

> One of Southwest Airline's strengths is its unique culture that includes a mandate for employees to have fun at work. The company's exceptional working atmosphere has resulted in unique and noteworthy success in the airline industry. "Find great people, love them, and they'll do marvelous things for your customers," says Brian Allen of Southwest's leadership training facility. Southwest has posted seven consecutive years of record profits, with the 1998 gain coming as other major airlines reported disappointing results. Its unionized work force has never seen a layoff. (*The Concord Monitor*, March 14, 1999, F-1)

nology? What are their target markets? What image are they trying to cultivate? Do they compete on price, quality, service, or convenience? Are they heavily in debt?

Determine what your competitors' strengths are, and learn from them. Avoid their weaknesses in your business, but be ready to confront them head-on with your marketing strategies.

For also knowledge itself is power.
FRANCIS BACON

You can give your business the competitive edge by offering service that's superior to that offered by your competitors. Good customer service means giving customers whatever it is that they need, whenever they need it.

Your customers are the lifeblood of your business. Make sure you treat them as such.

Take a look at all the ways your business interacts with customers, from the time someone calls your company requesting information to the time that a sale is complete. The way you and your employees answer your phones influences the way people feel about your company. A voice that is warm, welcoming, courteous, and knowledgeable makes people want to do business with you. A voice that's cold and uncaring will turn off even the most loyal of customers.

If your customer has a complaint, find out what the problem is. What can your company do to help a customer remedy his or her problem? Realize that people don't buy products and services. They buy

Larry Abramoff, owner of Tatnuck Bookseller in Worcester, Massachusetts, has not only survived in the face of competition—he has thrived. Since 1993, two Barnes & Nobles, a Borders and a Media Play opened within a few miles of his store—and the Internet has taken off as a big seller of books. Although sales dropped 20 percent in the first month of each big-name store's opening, Larry comes back stronger and stronger each time, by continuously and dramatically changing the size, scope and flavor of his business. (*The Wall Street Journal*, March 10, 1999, NE1)

> "As e-commerce explodes to an estimated $41 billion in sales by 2002, analysts say the quality of on-line customer service may determine whether a consumer shops at your site or surfs to another." (*American Demographics*, February 1999, page 36)

solutions to their problems, satisfactions of their wants and needs.

A man without a smiling face must not open a shop.
CHINESE PROVERB

Your relationship with a customer doesn't end once a sale is completed. Customer follow-up is one of the most important activities of every business' marketing efforts and, unfortunately, for many businesses, one of the most easily neglected.

In your marketing plan, make sure you've spelled out what your after-sale procedure is. Send a thank-you note or e-mail? Make a telephone call? Everyone who has contact with customers in your business should know what the procedure is and make sure that it's followed.

The easiest sale to make is one to a repeat customer. More than two-thirds of business in this country is lost due to lack of customer follow-up. What's more, it costs only one-sixth as much to sell something to an existing customer as it does to sell the same thing to a new person.

If you want good service, serve yourself.
SPANISH PROVERB

The cardinal rule of market planning is to put your customers first. To figure out how to do this, put yourself in their shoes and see how they view your products and services. If you can understand your products and services from their point of view, you can discover new ways to market your products and services, new target markets, new profitability.

For example, if a customer asked for a modified version of a standard product in your line, could you redesign it to his or her specifications? Who knows—maybe this new product would appeal to others in your market. This could be the first step to transforming valuable, informal market research into profits for your business.

Positioning your product or service is how you achieve your marketing goals. Positioning means finding and establishing your niche within your target market, so people know who you are and what you do. Through ongoing marketing efforts, you reinforce this kind of recognition.

Your position in the market depends on the unique selling proposition, or USP, of your product or service. What makes yours stand out from the competition? Is it quality? Price? Convenience? Style? Location? Professionalism? Your aim is to develop an image in the marketplace that you offer something special.

For example, what's really the difference between McDonald's, Wendy's, and Burger King? You can get burgers at all three relatively quickly and for around the same price. But on a given day, your kids may want the toy-of-the-week offered by Burger King, or you may want one of the lower-calorie wraps offered only at Wendy's. Here in New Hampshire, McDonald's occasionally offers lobster rolls—a lobster salad sandwich served at seafood restaurants on the New England seacoast—for "under four clams," almost half the price you'd pay anywhere else. These

The Dover Auto Center in Dover, New Hampshire, has the art of customer follow-up down to a science. After every appointment, customers get a phone call from a concerned representative wanting to know about the quality of the service. Whether the customer had an oil change or the transmission overhauled, the Dover Auto Center wants to make sure all its customers are satisfied and that they'll return when they have their next car problem.

In 1999 Pricewaterhouse-Coopers followed three other Big Five accounting firms in launching a block-buster $50 million ad campaign, the first major splash from the 1998 merger between Price Waterhouse and Coopers & Lybrand. "These firms are desperate to differentiate themselves because corporate clients tend to view them as one and the same," says a veteran industry watcher. "Great advertising fortunes have been built on distinguishing between Pepsi and Coke, and more great advertising fortunes are sure to be built on distinguishing between accounting firms." (*The Wall Street Journal*, March 9, 1999, B-18)

fast-food burger joints, which compete fiercely for your and my business, have successfully differentiated their fare from that offered by their competitor.

A hamburger by any other name costs twice as much.
EVAN ESAR

In addition to differentiating your products and services from those of the competition, you must also give your customers a reason to buy from you. Since people buy solutions to their problems and satisfaction of their wants and needs, remember to tout the benefits of your product or service —not its features.

Think of how over-the-counter pain relievers have succeeded here. Advil promises to relieve muscle pain, Bayer reminds you to take one of their aspirins to prevent heart attacks, Tylenol won't irritate your stomach, Excedrin will annihilate your headache, and you only have to take Aleve every eight hours.

You don't buy coal, you buy heat;
You don't buy circus tickets, you buy thrills;
You don't buy a paper, you buy news;
You don't buy spectacles, you buy vision;
You don't buy printing, you buy selling.
ANONYMOUS

You don't have to be a huge corporation like Bristol-Myers to create a brand name for your product or service. Brand names can be used by anyone willing to create them and smart enough to know their value.

People trust brand names, and they have confidence that a brand-name item will perform better than a nonbrand-name item. Since people want uniqueness and something they can trust, your job is to give it to them—to go that extra mile, give the extra service, give them that extra quality. Make sure your customers know they're getting the best and more than their money's worth.

If a man writes a better book, preaches a better sermon,
or makes a better mousetrap than his neighbor,
though he builds his house in the woods,
the world will make a beaten path to his door.

RALPH WALDO EMERSON

To position steel as the material of choice for the next millennium, steel makers realized that they had to get the message out to the consumers driving the cars and loading the washing machines. If they didn't understand steel's benefits, they might not demand the material in products they bought. And a drop in consumer demand would lead to a drop in orders from the industry's clients. (*American Demographics*, March 1999, page 56)

SECTION 2:

Learning about Your Market

4

Why Target Your Marketing?

To understand target marketing, think of all the people, near and far, who might conceivably buy your product. This is the total market. In order for people to buy from you, they must know that you provide that product, can provide it at a competitive price and in a manner convenient to them, and do all this to their satisfaction. However, you can afford to reach only a small fraction of this total market. Those persons in the market who are most likely to buy (they have the money), are most willing to buy (they want the product), are most accessible to you (your promotional messages reach them), and can most easily purchase from you (proximity is important, whether geographic or electronic) are your real target market.

How can you know who they are? Common sense provides a start. A blend of your insight and experience leavened with market research will help make the target market come alive. Trade sources can tell you about the individuals who buy your kind of product, their demographics and where they are, what they read and watch and listen to, their reasons for buying.

In the long run, men hit what they aim at.
HENRY DAVID THOREAU

Prodigy Communications' Spanish-language Internet-access service offers features targeted directly to users' tastes. "The market is large but underserved," says Prodigy's president David Trachtenberg. "We offer a seamless bilingual experience, all the way from sales and marketing to the registration process and even to picking an e-mail address." About 27 percent of U.S. Hispanic households have a personal computer at home and about 11 percent have Internet access. (*The Wall Street Journal*, April 6, 1999, B-6)

Niche marketing, the small business owners' best tool, is simple. You have to choose a niche that is large enough for you to grow and make a profit, yet small enough to defend against newcomers. (Your best defense is customer service, which retains customers. See Chapter 13.)

Ask yourself if your niche meets these simple criteria. If it does, fine. If not, keep looking.

A market niche is a small fragment of a larger market. You may choose a niche in many ways, but the best is to pick a niche that seems to be underserved by the products or services you offer. Suppose you sell a novel baby carrier on the Internet. You'd want your banners to appear on other sites frequented by new parents. iVillage.com bills itself on national television as the women's channel, and runs advertisements showing happy young mothers cooing over their offspring. Bingo: a good site to be linked with.

Why would this be a good niche? People comfortable with e-commerce tend to be "early adopters," marketing-speak for people willing to try something new. Their incomes are above average. If they frequent the sites that your banners appear on, you stand a fine chance of connecting with them.

You can't get all new parents, no matter how hard you try. To reach your niche, you have to know a lot about them: what sites they visit, what their hot buttons might be, what their expectations are. Focus on this small group and you can know what they want and how to serve them better than any of your competitors.

Small is beautiful.

E. F. SCHUMACHER

Target marketing does not imply that you focus on only one market niche. You can take a multiple target market stance, in which you identify two or more market segments with a need for your products. When Andy owned Upstart Publishing Company, he took this approach. His prime market consisted of several hundred banks with demonstrated interest in helping small businesses. This led to two other fast-growing markets: colleges and economic development agencies, including Small Business Development Centers. Each market called for a different approach. Within three years of adopting this tactic, commercial banks were dropped as the primary market and replaced by these faster-growing segments.

You can, of course, concentrate on a single target market. It depends on your business. A multiple target market spreads your efforts but provides protection against the cyclical nature of most markets. When banks lost interest in working with small businesses, the Small Business Administration and its many programs became more important to Upstart—and marketing to them took center stage.

The decision to approach several markets should not be taken lightly. It costs more. It strains resources, especially personnel. It is easier to be a force in a single niche than a force in several. It can be done—but be aware of the difficulties involved.

Never pontificate about the weather;
you may be all wet.

LEO ROSTEN

Is there a market for cars that cost $150,000 and up? With lots of people walking around with lots of money, Volkswagen, Mercedes, BMW, and Ford think so. They've invested heavily to get a piece of the very expensive car market, currently dominated by Ferrari, Rolls-Royce, and Bentley. If their plans pan out, supercar production could leap threefold to 18,000 by 2003. Volkswagen has plans to revive the 1930s-era Bugatti, for a cool $600,000. (*Forbes*, May 17, 1999)

> Carpe Diem, a specialty coffee roaster in Maine, initially followed a concentrated target market approach. They chose about a dozen gourmet stores on whom they lavished great care and attention rather than pursuing the 200 or more stores in their trading area. After two years, they came to the attention of Stonewall Kitchens, a fast-growing regional specialty foods company that offered to place Carpe Diem products in their 3,500 accounts. As of now, Carpe Diem is carefully expanding into this much larger market, maintaining their high quality and freshness through limiting the number of accounts they feel comfortable serving.

Limit your market size by segmenting your markets. You'll hear more about this in Chapter 5, and you'll hear it again after that. Small businesses cannot market their products to wide markets. The key is that the smaller your market, the larger the splash you can make. It is almost always better to be a large frog in a small pond than a tiny frog in Lake Superior.

First ask yourself: Who in the wide market is most likely to buy your product or service? These most likely customers will form clusters, groups with identifiable demographic, psychographic, or other characteristics. This defines a segment, which in turn may be further refined.

Next, who are *your* favorite clients? Chances are you have some customers who are a joy to work with, who trust your judgment and willingly spread the word about your excellent service. You can do much worse than use "like my favorite customers" as a segmenting tool. Andy's early customers were bankers, a group he was familiar with from being a banker himself.

Where do your profits come from? According to Pareto's principle, 80 percent of your profits come from 20 percent of your clients. Why not focus on this 20 percent, seek more like them, and forget the 80 percent who mainly bring you headaches?

If one part of your market is growing quickly, perhaps you should concentrate your efforts on that segment so you can grow with it. Conversely, if one segment of your market is shrinking, consider abandoning that segment.

Go where the dollars are. You have more choice over whom you serve than you may think. Willie Sutton, a bank robber of some note, said he robbed banks because that's where the money was. All things being equal, you should enter markets that aren't price sensitive. Leave the low end of the market to WalMart and Costco. Remember the principle that big fish in small ponds eat well.

> *Nature does nothing in vain, and*
> *more is vain when less will serve.*
>
> ISAAC NEWTON

Which approach do you use: a rifle or shotgun? Depends on what you are trying to shoot. If you are after a single large beast, use a rifle. If you are shooting for small game birds, use a shotgun. The same applies to marketing.

Think of the hundreds of millions of dollars expended by Coca-Cola and Pepsi in their cola wars. They aim for everyone—individual consumers, college cafeterias, fast-food joints, restaurant chains, commissaries. Everyone. Nationally and internationally. They have to use mass media, and their advertising has to be general. This is the ultimate shotgun approach. They know they won't get every customer they aim for, but they will get enough to justify the mass-market shotgun approach. Some ads will target market segments ("Pepsi generation" was a classic positioning campaign aimed at younger consumers) but overall their approach is to every possible cola drinker.

Kodak is targeting "tween" girls, aged nine to 15 years old in a marketing campaign. Company studies show that tween girls are more likely than boys to own a camera and that pictures are more important possessions to teen girls than their own pets. Kodak will consider the campaign a success if it garners added sales of several hundred million dollars of the $130 billion in annual spending attributed to Generation Y, those born between 1978 and 1998. (*The Wall Street Journal*, June 15, 1999)

SoHo soda's founder Sophia Collier schlepped her product store to store in New York City, selling broken cases, even single bottles, to the stores she had targeted. She later sold her company for $25 million to a behemoth, proving that a rifle can be more effective than a shotgun for the small operator.

There is room for regional products like Moxie, Royal Crown, and birch beer, specialty products such as Schweppes ginger beer or bitter lemon. Plenty of room for target marketers who know enough to spot a niche, then exploit it.

Fortune favors the brave.

VIRGIL

"Best customers" lead to target markets. Who are your favorite (not necessarily largest or most profitable) customers? What do you like about them? Let's suppose that once you think about these customers you find that they pay quickly, don't quibble about price, appreciate your efforts to serve them better than the competition, and are frequent purchasers.

Now: What do these folks have in common? Where do they live? What do they earn? How do they like to be treated? What do they pay attention to?

The next step (after looking for these common links) is to find out if there are enough people like them in your trading area to provide a viable market.

Can you imagine how much fun it would be to serve only people you like and trust? Worth the effort? You bet it is!

The Internet is made for target marketing. E-commerce is exploding fast, becoming a major retailing channel with stunning speed.

Consider Eric Stites, president of Yaz Inc. He spotted an interesting target market: men who have difficulty finding the right unique present for their women. Talk about a huge market! He decided to use the Web as his main marketing effort, figuring that men who use the Web would be prequalified as prospects interested in getting advice about jewelry and craft items.

Visit his site: *www.yaz.com* to see how a low-budget e-commerce site works. His site gets some 3,000 hits a day. That's the functional equivalent of 3,000 qualified prospects walking into his "storefront" every day!

If only I had known,
I should have become a watchmaker.
ALBERT EINSTEIN

Understanding the perceptions of your target market is the goal of your market research. This research will not be too expensive if you limit your market. You can learn what moves your target market best if it is small. A market with thousands of people in it is hard to describe except in general terms. General terms and a dollar may get you a cup of coffee, but it won't create customers.

Don't understand market research? Use a college near you. You'll be surprised how effective they can be.

What we have to learn to do, we learn by doing.
ARISTOTLE

What should you find out about your target markets and their perceptions of your company, products,

In a nationwide listing of search firms, McCormack & Associates is the only one to list recruiting of homosexuals as a specialty. Founded in 1994, the company grew to nearly half a million dollars in billings in five years and now recruits gay, minority, disabled and straight men and women sensitive to homosexual issues. (*The Wall Street Journal*, March 16, 1999)

and services? Everything you can, certainly more than your competitors are willing to learn.

Here is what you *must* learn:

- Who are these people? This is where demographics and similar tools help.
- What do they buy? They buy toast, not toasters; quarter-inch holes, not drills.
- When do they make their purchases? Once in a lifetime (an engagement ring) or several times a week (groceries)? Do they buy during the day, in the morning, in the evening, any old time?
- How do they buy the kinds of things you sell? In a store, through e-commerce, direct mail, by phone?
- How do they like to pay? Cash or charge, credit card, store card? Extended terms?
- Why do they purchase your goods and services? Why from you? Why not?
- How can you differentiate yourself from the competition? What makes you different *in their eyes*? (Not in yours!)
- Most important of all: What do your customers and prospects perceive to be value in your goods and services? Do they cherish fast delivery, courteous service, wide product lines?

Then provide it. You'll become rich and famous.

Upstart, Andy's publishing company, first looked at commercial banks as its market. At the time, there were more than 14,000 commercial banks in the country ranging from Chase Manhattan down to tiny unit banks in Montana. It's hard to see what these had in common. For less than $1,000 plus use of Andy's 800-lines, a group of University of New Hampshire MBA students under the tutelage of Starr Schlobohm, a veteran marketing professor, quickly redefined Andy's market as 500 banks, all clearly committed to working with small business owners. The next step was paring this list to 200 banks. You can learn a lot about 200 prospects—the names of the players, their thoughts, their aspirations, their spending limits, what they really wanted. Most of them wanted to be promoted, so Andy and his sales force produced a "hero kit" to help these prospects become advocates of Upstart's newsletter programs within their banks.

There is no subject so old that something new cannot be said about it.
FYODOR MIKHAILOVICH DOSTOEVSKY

Bankers and other investors will ask you what your market share is. This sounds more difficult to answer than it really is.

First, determine the number of prospects in your target market. If your target market is defined by households in your trading area with family incomes greater than $60,000 per year (for example), a visit to the library will yield the census data you need. *Sales and Marketing Management*, a magazine for marketers, contains this kind of information in their July issue for every county or SMSA in the country. Ask your librarian for help—he or she is a trained researcher.

Second, determine the rate of usage of your product or service. Is it weekly (groceries), monthly, annually, once in a great while?

Third, determine the potential annual purchase. Let's see…5,000 families buying my gizmo twice a year at $200 a pop…that's $2 million per year (5,000 × 2 × $200).

Fourth, estimate the percentage of this annual sum you have or can attain. If you can get 25 percent of it, you should be selling $500,000 per year. This equates to 1,250 households.

Nobody gets 100 percent of market share. A 25 percent share is considered dominant—with this share you'll be a major contender, and will usually be considered by all purchasers as a possible supplier. You use market share as a measure of how well you are

After 113 years of direct selling, Avon Products is entering the mall to target the 20 to 30 million women not buying its products today. Avon is positioning kiosks in pricier neighborhoods that may be beyond the reach of its middle-America reps. And teenagers, who average 27 percent more mall visits than other shoppers, have noticed Avon's allowance-friendly $6 lipsticks. (*American Demographics*, "Avon Calling," April 1999)

With $1 billion in 1998 revenue, adult Web sites are a market David Shaw wants to cash in on. By using his prepaid cards, akin to those for long-distance calling, customers could avoid using credit cards and preserve their anonymity. Shaw hopes to have every corner store and truck stop sell his card, and hopes to rope in 100,000 monthly card carriers within 12 months. That would bring in $12 million in annual revenue, and Shaw has plans for overseas expansion. (*Forbes*, June 14, 1999, page 45)

doing, as a goal, and as an important piece of market planning information.

If you don't know your market share, you have a homework assignment: Determine your share of the target market.

In a strong position, even a coward is a lion.
HINDU PROVERB

What is the target market doing? If you have five percent of a $10 million market, or sales of $500,000, it makes a huge difference to your plans to know whether the market is growing, stable, or shrinking.

Five percent of a growing market calls for aggressive expansion plans. Growing markets attract competitors, so "business as usual" will cost you market share very quickly. Fortunately, this kind of market is very attractive to investors, so capital to grow will be available. Look at the way Internet stocks boomed in 1999.

Five percent of a shrinking market calls for examining your investment options. Though it is possible to thrive in a shrinking market, long term it may not be in your best interests. Why own 100 percent share of the buggy whip or BetaMax market?

Five percent of a stable market offers more options. If the stability represents a correction in the market, be aggressive. If it presages a mature market, consider gaining market share by acquiring competitors. This is called the "Pac-man strategy," named after the video game. Good examples are the growth of giant realtors such as Coldwell Banker or ambulance services by American Response driven by buying out local companies and bringing them under the cover of a nationwide firm.

Business is more exciting than any game.
LORD BEAVERBROOK

Beloit, Wisconsin-based Newell is a company famous for "Newellizations." In 10 years, it bought 75 mediocre, smallish companies and polished them up by eliminating the least valuable products, employees, factories and customers. Most of its targets had strong brand names (Sharpie markers, BenzOmatic torches, Rubbermaid's Little Tykes toys) but bad customer service. (*Forbes*, May 31, 1999, page 118)

5

Who Are Your Current Customers?

Who buys your products and services? You can never know too much about your customers, both current and prospective. If you know who your customers are and why they buy from you, you'll have an easier time selling to them once, selling to them again, finding more customers like them, and out-performing your competitors.

Where do you get information about your customers? From market research, which reveals facts and figures that transform your marketing goals from wishful thinking into a concrete action plan. Although your hunches are important starting points, they have to be substantiated. "I have a hunch that there's a big market for ..." and "I feel that we can double sales by..." are two of the most common traps small business owners fall into. Bolster your intuition with hard facts and solid numbers.

Some market research is informal and can be done by you and your staff. Some is available at your library or from government agencies. Some is best left to professional marketing consultants, who can get certain information more quickly and less expensively than you can. If your budget is tight, check with local business schools. Marketing professors sometimes do consulting work, as do MBA students.

Alison Gerlach, president of City Access Providers, aims her "quality of life" concierge services to employers anxious to retain talented employees. Her pitch? Suppose a firm is competing with rivals for hiring the best and the brightest among recent graduates. A firm using her company would have an advantage. "If you're asking someone to work for you 12 to 14 hours a day," she says, "this is a way to indicate to the staff that you care about the quality of their personal lives." (*The Boston Globe*, March 11, 1999)

The sole purpose of business is to create a customer.
PETER DRUCKER

Detailed information about your current customers allows you to improve your marketing efforts and specify the groups you're targeting.

If you sell to individuals, what is your customer's age, gender, income, education level, profession, stage in the life cycle? Does he or she own a home? What do they read, watch, listen to? Which media do they prefer? What do they buy? When do they buy? How do they buy? And, last but not least, why do they buy? This last question has been called a "$64,000 question" because people buy for so many different reasons. In general, consumers act emotionally rather than rationally, and respond to the same stimulus in different ways.

If you sell to industrial markets, who are they? What are their sales levels? Where are they located? Who makes their buying decisions? Which market segment buys which of your products, and what information can these people give to you?

Look for more detailed information on market research in Chapter 7.

People who understand consumer behavior make more money in the stock market than professional stock pickers who rely on financial numbers. If you like the store, chances are you'll love the stock.
PETER LYNCH

Answers to these questions help you home in on who your best customers and prospects are, what they want from a business like yours, how they perceive your products and services, how you can profitably meet their needs, and what the potential for this market is. This is what's called "market segmentation," a method of organizing and categorizing people or organizations who buy from you.

For example, Procter & Gamble knows that different market segments buy its Crest toothpaste. It therefore markets Crest with different advertising and marketing campaigns to children, senior citizens, and Hispanics.

Market segmentation is very logical. It is based on the premise that no single marketing strategy is appropriate for all possible buyers. Your objective is to find people or organizations with similar needs, wants, and behaviors, and design a marketing program that's appropriate for that particular group.

Birds of a feather flock together.

ARISTOTLE

Market segmentation takes the core benefits of products or services and seeks to find how many people are likely to want each benefit, how much they would be willing to pay for it, and where they'd like to buy it from. Initially, when Ford Motor Company introduced its Model T, it had a standard engine and components, and was offered in "any color you wanted as long as it was black." When

Not only does Unity Marketing of Reinholds, Pennsylvania, know that the market for collectible plush teddy bears has grown significantly since the early 1990s—they know exactly who's buying. Most buyers are women, but men represent 15 percent of the market. Twenty-seven percent of plush collectors are aged 35 to 44, and 35 percent are aged 45 to 54. Sixty-one percent of the collectors have attended college, and 56 percent of collectors have annual incomes of $45,000 or more—helpful, since the average collectible teddy can cost up to $90 (*American Demographics*, "A Bear Market for Teddies," February 1996).

some owners began replacing the bodies with truck beds and making the engine more powerful, Ford realized it could make more money offering these alterations as factory alternatives and charging a little more for them. Consequently, Ford's focus changed from trying to produce cars as cheaply as possible to producing cars that were as desirable as possible.

Consumers are usually prepared to pay a premium price for a product or service that closely fits their needs. Identifying a target group and knowing its needs allows you to position your product in your target group's minds and adopt an appropriate promotional strategy with appealing ads. When you know what your target group thinks of as "good value," you can determine a pricing strategy. And when you know where your target group shops, you can develop a distribution strategy.

The buyer has need of a hundred eyes,
the seller of but one.

ITALIAN PROVERB

The purpose of market segmentation is to form a mental picture of your ideal customer. The bigger your segment, the greater your profit potential will be.

For a segment to be worth pursuing, you must be able to measure it, to access it in some identifiable way, and to make money doing so. Your product or service must meet your customers' needs better than the

In 1999, e-entrepreneur Jon Rittenberg launched Simply-Modern.com, which sells the kind of upscale curiosities Boston shoppers might find in small Back Bay shops. Among his offerings: CD racks and a $74 brushed-metal lamp similar to those spotted on the TV show *Ally McBeal*. Rittenberg sees his company as the exact opposite of on-line bookseller Amazon.com, which sells a commodity product to the masses and competes on low prices. He sells around 90 unique products to a very small niche—young professionals with an artistic bent, people who earn lots of money but who have little time to spend it. (*The Boston Globe*, March 24, 1999, D-1)

competition so that your customers perceive your business as giving them the best value for their money.

Saddle your dreams afore you ride 'em.
MARY WEBB

There are basically five ways to segment a market. Demographics looks at the group's gender, age, income, family size, occupation, salary, lifestyle, and so on. (Demography is the study of human populations in terms of size, density, distribution, growth, and vital statistics.) Psychographics looks at a group's behavior patterns, attitudes, and expectations. Geographics is based on where people live, whereas behavioral segmentation looks at what people do. Sociocultural segmentation takes into account religion, national origin, race, social class, and marital status.

For example, if you were in the clothing business, you could segment demographically by marketing to 18- to 24-year-olds who buy bell-bottomed jeans and big, clunky shoes. Or you might cater to infants and toddlers, or women with lots of disposable income to spend on clothes. If you segmented behaviorally, you might specialize in clothing for golfers, hikers, or those climbing the corporate career ladder. If you segmented geographically, you could offer clothing for people living in warmer climates. Sociocultural segmentation would mean providing saris for Indians, muu-muus for Hawaiians, habits for nuns, and so on. Psychographic segmentation might mean appealing

Fancy bacon from North Country Smokehouse in Claremont, New Hampshire, has been served to the Pope and *New York Times* health writer Jane Brody. Other clients include The Four Seasons Hotel in New York and the MGM Grand in Las Vegas. Specialty products are shipped to Hong Kong, Tokyo and Melbourne and are served to first-class passengers on Air Singapore. North Country survives by targeting the high end of the market, where buyers will pay more for exactly what they want. Owner Mike Satzow says his bacon "is perceived as the best in the industry." Customers are extremely loyal, and new accounts are often picked up when a high-power chef changes jobs. (*The Concord Monitor*, March 23, 1999)

David Carter, owner of Carter's Cross Country Ski Centers in Maine, pursues customers who take their canine pals along on romps in the woods. He offers groomed trails dedicated to dog owners, known in his business as "loop de poop" trails. Carter decided to allow dogs at his ski centers after being asked by many customers. He estimates that this decision boosted business by five to ten percent, and he's never had to confiscate a doggie pass for misbehavior. (*The Concord Monitor*, February 16, 1999, B-3)

to people who hit the upscale stores when they know a sale's going on.

A lady is known by the product she endorses.
OGDEN NASH

What's the best way to segment your business's market? It really depends on the type of information you're looking for and the type of business you have.

If you specialized in home improvements, you would most likely segment your market on a geographic basis. You'd target people living in certain neighborhoods—in homes more than 40 years old, say. There'd be no point in marketing your services to people living in the five-year-old subdivision down the road or at renters who don't even own their own homes. They don't need what you have to offer. You'd want to further refine your search to affluent executives and professionals, comfortable middle-agers, and prosperous retirees who'd be most likely to have the disposable income to spend on your services—certainly not young newlyweds or people in low-income areas.

If you had a cycle shop, you wouldn't care how old your customers are or what their occupation is (demographic data), or whether they were Asian or Hispanic (sociocultural data). All you'd be concerned with is whether they like to go bicycling (behavioral segmentation).

If you ran a vegetarian restaurant, you'd be fairly certain that your customers are partial to environmental causes, recycle their trash, and probably own a bike instead of a car if they lived in a city (psychographics).

If the shoe fits, wear it.
VARIATION OF A 17TH-CENTURY ENGLISH PROVERB

Segmenting your market helps you figure out the best way to reach customers. Should the home-improvement business do a mass-mailing to everyone in its county, which could be expensive and time consuming, or deliver flyers to everyone in carefully selected neighborhoods? For the bicycle shop, an ad in the local paper or donating a bike to the hospital's auction might be just the ticket to getting the word out about its products and services. The vegetarian restaurant could put posters in the local health-food store.

As the saying goes, there's no point in trying to sell ice to the Eskimos, when there's a ready market in Florida. Know who your market is, where they are, and what the best way is to reach them. Don't waste your precious time and resources heading down the wrong path.

Demographic segmentation is probably the most common method of segmentation. The statistics are fairly reliable because if we know how many 40-year-olds we have today, we can predict how many 50-year-olds we'll have in 10 years. We know what the death rate is for people in their 40s, due to disease, accidents, and natural disasters, and it's easy to get accurate information regarding the immigration rate.

Now that non-Europeans make up more than 25 percent of American society, ethnic marketing has become more and more important for businesses. Opportunities abound, as African Americans' purchasing power totals around $500 billion, Hispanics' around $350 billion and Asian Americans' around $150 billion. The catch for tapping the great profit potential of these markets: developing a pitch that's right on target. (*Success*, April 1999, page 38)

The Wall Street Journal runs an ad for its Golf Corner section that says, "1.5 million *Wall Street Journal* golfers do not read *Golf Digest*, *Golf Magazine*, or *Golf for Women*." The paper offers businesses targeting golfers an affluent audience devoted to the game, but unreachable via other publications.

Aside from age, family structure issues can play an important role in some businesses' marketing decisions. People today are marrying later than they did in their parent's generation. More women are working outside the home and postponing childbearing. There are more one-child families than there were 25 years ago. Think of how all these trends affect child-care businesses, restaurants, caterers, housekeepers, personal service businesses, pet-sitters, elder-care, and so on. The list is a long one.

I have often admired the mystical way of Pythagoras,
and the secret magic of numbers.
Sir Thomas Browne

Psychographics is used less frequently than demographics because getting the necessary research is complex and time consuming, and relies heavily on the judgment of the researcher. Psychographics can help to tell us what people will buy since it relates consumer lifestyles to consumers' purchasing behavior. An example of this approach is the VALS (value and lifestyle structure) created by researchers at Stanford Research Institute in the early 1980s to describe nine different lifestyle options.

This research helped Manufacturers Hanover Trust Company in New York identify six psychographic groups within one demographic segment, the baby boomers. The result was a successful marketing campaign that used only one slogan, "We realize your potential," to appeal to the six different mindsets.

You will probably find that you sell most profitably to certain segments and poorly to others. Think of the 80/20 rule which states that 80 percent of your profits come from 20 percent of your customers. If you can get a good handle on who that profitable 20 percent is and who the unprofitable 80 percent is, your business will prosper.

Eighty percent of your results come from 20 percent of your efforts.
PARAPHRASED FROM VILFREDO PARETO

Certain psychographic changes in attitude and behavior have taken place as a result of demographic changes in the birth rate. The baby boomers were born in the 15 or so years after World War II, a time of rising prosperity when young couples were confident about starting families. The boomers experienced increased personal freedom and had greater expectations than their parents. They tend to buy more and save less than previous generations.

Baby busters were born between 1964 and 1980, a time of falling birth rates, falling standards of living, oil crises, a rise of one-parent or both-working families. They tend to be heavy consumers, hard workers, educated, ambitious, selfish, and determined to succeed financially. Theirs is the generation of the yuppies (young, urban professionals). Many are DINKs (double income, no kids), SINKs (single income, no kids), or SITCOMs (single income, two children, outrageous mortgage).

After more than 25 years, a Houston-based death-services company is using demographics to expand its $1.1 billion business. Service Corporation International (SCI), the world's largest funeral-service company, spends $200,000 a year on demographic research from the Census Bureau and the National Center for Health Statistics. The information they gather helps them target under-served markets for development of new funeral facilities. Before they began using demographics, SCI grew by purchasing existing funeral homes. (*American Demographics*, May 1995)

As the nation's 76 million baby boomers age, there's a growing interest in long-term care insurance. Such policies protect against the risk of incurring costly custodial care at home or at a nursing facility should the policyholder become disabled. Neither Medicare or Medigap covers these costs, which can run $40,000 a year or more. Only a handful of companies offer the coverage as part of their employee-benefit packages. An estimate by Portland, Maine-based UNUM Corporation, a major provider of long-term care insurance, estimates the market at $20 billion, versus the barely $1 billion in policies sold so far. (*Business Week*, March 29, 1999, B-4)

Woopies are well-off older people over age 65. They have generous pensions, substantial savings and investments, and relatively low outflow of cash. They spend more, on average, on their homes, vacations, and financial services. Companies such as Saga Holidays have tapped this market very successfully by catering to the elderly. It ensures that its clients rarely have to carry their own luggage any distance. Their vacations are not cheap, but they are just what the over-55 market wants.

The U.S. Census Bureau (*www.census.gov*) is a wealth of information on our population and its demographics. You can get national and state population profiles; national, state, and county statistics on age data; demographic data on any number of countries in the world; and even information on who owns and uses computers. Check it out!

Be curious always! For knowledge will not acquire you; you must acquire it.

SUDIE BLACK

The other demographic trend that's impossible to ignore is the aging of America. The U.S. population aged 65 and over will double to nearly 70 million in 2030, and the over-85 age group is the fastest growing segment of the population, according to government statistics. People are living longer thanks to medical advances and healthier lifestyles. Even younger people are taking better care of themselves, as evidenced by the skyrocketing sales of health and fitness products. Spending on leisure pursuits has also hit new high levels, thanks to retirees with more time on their hands.

How does the aging of America affect your business?

There is no cure for birth or death
save to enjoy the interval.
GEORGE SANTAYANA

As the 76 million baby boomers begin to age and die, the nation's death rate will soar by nearly 40 percent, according to Hillenbrand Industries, the nation's biggest casket maker. But boomers are choosing cremation and other low-cost funeral options: only 15.2 percent of people who died were cremated in 1987. The number jumped to 23.6 percent in 1997 and is expected to hit 42 percent by 2010. Hillenbrand has reacted by offering a full line of urns and cremation caskets. Although the casket market is flat, Hillenbrand continues to grow market share because it has embraced cremation. (*The Wall Street Journal*, March 22, 1999, B-4)

6 Who Are Your Competitors?

What is a competitive edge? Is it temporary or should it be sustainable, a permanent leg up on the competition in some important (that is, to your customers and prospects) way?

All business is competitive. If you don't have competitors, take it as a warning sign—it means either that there is no viable business opportunity or that you are the pioneer, the first to see a market where others have not.

The business arena is comprised of a few winners (who consistently make profits, grow, capture market share, provide increasing value to their markets), a few losers (who don't make money and sooner or later fail), and the largest group of all, those who may or may not be winners this year.

Sounds simple. The consistent winners don't stay on top by accident. They have an edge, something they excel at doing. Experts call this their "core competency." WalMart's extraordinary distribution system is a great example. Their network of vast distribution centers linked with state-of-the-art sales and inventory information means they can shift fast-moving items to stores that need them within hours. Not days.

They developed their distribution system carefully and at great expense. It provides a sustainable edge nearly impervious to competitors because the cost of creating such a system from scratch is prohibitive.

The Lazarus Department store in Indianapolis is now home to the St. Vincent Women's Center. There, in a set of offices off the store's bathing suit department, women can get screened for breast cancer for an initial fee of $75, which can be charged to their Lazarus credit card. The center also tests for osteoporosis for an additional $25. "The big message is convenience," says a Lazarus spokesperson. "Now women can add a screening to their shopping lists." (*The Wall Street Journal,* June 8, 1999, B-4B)

By the time WalMart's competition could see what WalMart was doing, it was already too late to play catch-up. WalMart's owners, managers, and employees recognize the value of their distribution system and constantly seek ways to improve it. Customers value it too, though perhaps unwittingly: Things are less expensive at WalMart. Consistently. Every day. WalMart uses this core competency to maintain their overwhelming competitive edge in their mass markets.

What is your core competency? Can you turn it into a long-term competitive edge?

Wisdom denotes the pursuing of
the best ends by the best means.

FRANCIS HUTCHESON

If you know where you stand vis-à-vis your competition, you can do something about it. You can capitalize on your relative strengths, turning them into a competitive edge. If you have weaknesses (and who doesn't?), you can eliminate them, change personnel or systems or both, find ways to avoid the dangers that competitive weaknesses present.

How do you establish your position? Some footwork is needed. One way is to use a form such as shown here. Suppose your three most direct competitors are Nightline, Delphi, and Rerun.

	YOU	NIGHTLINE	DELPHI	RERUN
MARKET SHARE	12%	15%	26%	14%
PRODUCT LINE	above average	below average	leader	don't know
MARKET POSITION	slow growth	losing share	leader	fast growth
MAIN STRENGTH	training	long industry experience	deepest knowledge of industry	rapid innovation
MAIN WEAKNESS	lack capital for growth	personnel turnover	too much adminis-tration	sometimes distracted by new ideas

In this hypothetical example, there is a clear leader, a company losing ground, and two companies moving up. This will yield you a lot more information than a simple

weak>————X————————<strong

continuum. And information, at the end of the day, makes all the difference.

I don't meet the competition. I crush it.

CHARLES REVSON

All smart companies (or smart managers) make a point of knowing what their competition is up to. One aspect of this is reverse engineering. Suppose you make high-end desk radios. You'd be foolish

Yachtstore.com, which expects to gross $10 million in 1999, doesn't have an office. Its 3,000 pages make it the Internet's largest virtual yachting brochure. "Yachting follows the money," says co-founder Carlos Echeverria, "and right now that's in Silicon Valley. They prefer our way of doing business on the Web." Low-overhead Internet shopping offers privacy and a discreet way for landlubbers to ask dumb questions. (*Forbes*, May 3, 1999, page 96)

McDonald's officials wouldn't comment on Burger King's new look for the 21st century. But employees of the prototype, which sits across the street from a McDonald's in Oak Brook, Illinois, said they spotted a McDonald's supervisor parked in their drive-through, which wasn't even completed at the time. (*The Wall Street Journal*, April 14, 1999, B-1)

not to keep up with Bose and Kloss and the other key competitors. Their technologies may or may not be proprietary, protected by patents—that's another problem, but the chances are that 95 percent of the technology is publicly available. Some speakers, transistors, microchips, electronic thingies, a box to hold it, knobs or buttons for fine tuning, and voilà, you've got a radio!

How does it all fit together? To find out, take the radios apart. Figure out how they did it. Can you improve on the process? Use a different process to obtain better results? Are they riding an obsolete technology? Are they using microchip technologies that defy analysis? Where do they get them?

Remember: The more you know, the better off you will be competitively.

We can't cross a bridge until we come to it: but I always like to lay down a pontoon ahead of time.

BERNARD BARUCH

Here are some more ways to look at your competition. Go to school on them to see what they do well (can you use their kinds of systems or do better than they?) and what they do poorly (what traps can you avoid?). Start with some baseline competitive information.

Don't rush this. Your aim is to be thorough and factual. There are no shortcuts. Your more able competitors will be doing this kind of analysis even if it is tedious, a task easily postponed and forgotten.

Get these baseline facts:

1. Names and addresses of competitors
2. Names and roles of key players
3. How they position their goods in your markets
4. What markets they target
5. Number of employees
6. Sales in dollars and units
7. Market share
8. Key customers
9. Distribution patterns
10. Years in business

Do you know these things? If not, how come?

Ignorance of one's ignorance is the greatest ignorance.
PETER'S ALMANAC

Supplier relationships are a good source of competitive intelligence. There's nothing sneaky or immoral about gathering and using information—it's part of being in business. Think of the way baseball teams scout their opposition.

You and your competitors probably share suppliers. These may be generic (office supplies, banking services) or more specific to your industry. If you have good supplier relationships (you better since there's every reason to keep suppliers on your side), you can ask if so-and-so is a customer. You may pick up some ideas, hints of what the competition is going to do. Suppose the salesperson tells you that your number-

Eager to dethrone Sears as the mass retailer most aggressively courting Hispanics in Los Angeles, the Target discount chain is remodeling stores and refashioning its merchandise mix. Target appointed 20-year veteran Jane Hanzalik as ethnic merchandiser to increase its appeal to Hispanics. She read books about Hispanic consumers, attended seminars, and visited stores known for catering to them. When she visited a nearby Sears, she admired the breadth of its children's department—crucial because Hispanics tend to have larger-than-average families—but felt that the store needed refurbishing and had too few bilingual signs. (*The Wall Street Journal*, April 12, 1999, A-1)

one competitor has just placed an unusually large order for some item. Wouldn't this be helpful to know?

Bankers and other professionals tend to be more tight-lipped. They should be. If a competitor is getting new financing or making a major purchase, there will be a public record, a bulk sales agreement, for example, or a public offering. There are plenty of ways to get this information, ranging from do-it-yourself perusal of financial newspapers, to hiring a clipping service, to using an Internet search engine like *www.infoseek.com.* Check trade publications, chamber of commerce newsletters, help-wanted ads, and keep an ear open for gossip.

Incidentally, you can ask your banker to make an introduction to a competitor; being a go-between is part of the banker's role. Sharing information may be of benefit to you and your competition—and to your suppliers and bankers.

Competitor files on your five most direct competitors yield big dividends for a small amount of effort. You'll have direct competitors. Even nonprofits compete for talent, donor money, and community acceptance.

Competitor files are simple manila folders, one for each competitor on whom you wish to keep close tabs. Keep this process simple by limiting yourself to no more than five or six competitors.

Using these files is easy. Pop in every bit of information you can glean. Clip their advertisements, date and file them. Toss in any filings, notices of new debt, legal proceedings, articles about their products, personnel, anything that gives you a handle on their positioning and pricing strategies. Don't ignore want ads; they help you estimate growth, key player turnover, even hints of future plans. If they use radio or television, jot down the message and your impression of whom they are trying to reach. If you attend the same trade association meetings or conventions, get their flyers and other collateral material such as facilities brochures. This is all grist for your mill.

Competitor files take only minutes to set up and maintain.

Now, put these files to work. Once a month spend a few minutes reviewing each file. Look for patterns. You'll soon know your competition better than they know themselves. You can be objective, they cannot. After six months, look around and see if a new file should be added, or if you can delete an old one.

You can observe a lot by just watching.
YOGI BERRA

Most of the time, you will be aware of your direct competitors, and though they may be a constant concern, they are unlikely to put you out of business. Your indirect competitors, those who compete for your target markets' dollars with vastly different or unrelated products or services, may pose a more severe threat since you don't tend to notice what they are doing until it's too late.

Pretend for a moment that you run a local video store. Your trading area contains six other video stores, two in supermarkets, two franchised mall-based outlets that vigorously promote the videos of

Coors brewing company learned the hard way to never underestimate its competitors. During the heady days of the early 1970s, Coors dominated every market it was in. But it stood little chance of cracking the Eastern market unless it increased marketing expenditures and established breweries closer to those markets. Even its captive and cherished Western markets were vulnerable to the aggressive efforts of major competitors. By 1981, Coors's share of the California market had dropped to 20 percent from a high of nearly 38 percent in 1972. (Robert F. Hartley, *Marketing Mistakes*, New York: John Wiley & Sons, Inc., 1992, page 75)

1998 was the biggest box office year in the history of the movie industry. That motion pictures did so well flew in the face of forecasts dating back to the early years of television. In the '50s, everyone said television was going to kill movie-going. Then videocassettes, cable, and satellite transmissions were going to turn theaters into big empty rooms. "Most families don't want to be tethered every evening to an electronic box, no matter how sweeping its reach," said Jack Valenti, chair of the Motion Picture Association. He contends that competition has actually increased theater attendance, because people cannot duplicate the epic viewing experience in their homes. (*The Concord Monitor*, March 20, 1999, A-7)

the week, an "adult" video (why do they call them adult?) store, and one store specializing in foreign and classic titles. These are your direct competitors. The adult and specialty stores have their own target markets, which don't severely overlap yours—but the other four all pursue the family and non-X-rated fans.

Guess who might put you out of business? Your cable television or satellite dish company. Technological capacities already permit movies-on-demand via cable or satellite, and together with the more familiar HBO and similar extra-price movie channels form a formidable competitor. The Internet promises to be another threat. In five years, you may be downloading movies from any number of Internet sources both national and foreign, ranging from the media giants like Disney and Time Warner to tiny independent art-movie houses.

Pay attention to your enemies, for they are
the first to discover your mistakes.

ANTISTHENES

Check out the "user-friendliness" of your competition. These days we all expect prompt, courteous, capable service—and when we don't get it, we move our trade elsewhere.

Many retailers routinely shop the competition to get a feel for the courtesy and knowledgeability of their sales staff, the condition of their premises, the freshness of their merchandise. Restaurant owners make a habit of visiting their competition to sample the food and service. Lawyers check up on other lawyers, carefully and discreetly in order to avoid legal entanglements, but they check up nonetheless. Most law firms are interested in getting a larger share of the legal pie even if they pretend otherwise.

Almost every business claims to put their customers' interests at the heart of operations. Very few really do. Most use gimmicks ("Have a nice day!") but don't go to the trouble of really putting their customers first. But what a positioning tool this can be! Among things to look for (in your own shop as well as other owners' shops) are:

- Courtesy, always a result of strict and careful training
- Safe, clean, well-lit premises
- Convenient access, including parking or proximity to good public transportation
- Hours of operation that meet the needs of the customer, not the pleasure of the owner

Close attention to these kinds of details is the core of customer service.

Happy the man who has been able to know the reasons for things.

VIRGIL

If there is one thing to learn about your competitors, it is this: How do they try to position their wares in the minds of their target markets? Wee Willie Keeler, a famous ballplayer for the Baltimore Orioles back in the

Cuisinart, the innovator of the food processor, badly underestimated the demand for convenience and compactness when Sunbeam launched its Oskar in 1985. The compact food processor/blender sold for $60, as opposed to Cuisinart's $200+ price. That year Sunbeam sold 700,000 Oskars, 25 percent of all food processors, and Cuisinart's volume share dropped from 20 percent to 10. In the fall of 1986, Cuisinart responded with a $40 Mini-mate grinder/chopper. But the damage had been done—consumers no longer saw Cuisinart as a cutting-edge innovator and neither did retailers. (Peter R. Dickson, *Marketing Management*, Fort Worth: The Dryden Press, 1994, page 258)

gaslight era, said his hitting strategy was simple: "I hit 'em where they ain't." This got him into the Hall of Fame.

Know what your competition is doing. Most likely they are plugging along with no particular strategy beyond business as usual. Fine; that's helpful information. Businesses acquire a form of commercial momentum over time. People know of them and are used to trading with them. Momentum is powerful, but you can turn their strength into your profit by carefully positioning yourself against them. More on this in Chapter 7.

Those few competitors who thoughtfully target your market and have adopted a positioning strategy pose a much different problem. Everyone claims "quality, customer centered, committed to excellence" and so on. Some will use price, or snob appeal, or convenience, or superb service as their claim to fame. Now that you know what they are doing, you can emulate Wee Willie and hit 'em where they ain't.

What holes are left unfilled in your markets? What positions have not been staked out? Would a sale aimed at Company X's core customers work? How about a value position such as "service plus warranty"?

This is virgin territory for whorehouses.

AL CAPONE

Use this form to get a quick read on your position vis-à-vis your competitors.

CUSTOMER WANTS	COMPETITOR PROVIDES	YOU PROVIDE
Quality		
Exclusivity		
Low price		
High price		
Wide product line*		
Deep product line		
Product service		
Reliability		
Warranty		
Delivery		
Location		
Information		
Rapid availability		
Credit services		
Accessories		
Well-trained staff		
Customer service		

Andy's favorite positioning for a printshop came from Philadelphia: "fast turn-around, mediocre quality." Their target market was more interested in fast turnaround than in high quality, knowing that in printing you can get one or the other but not both.

Use this to compare yourself to each competitor in turn.

How do your business adversaries advertise their goods and services? Careful analysis of their advertisements will pay off.

What message are they trying to get across? This is where you look for their positioning strategy.

What image are they conveying? Up market? Down market? Just plain folks?

At whom are they aiming their advertisements? What market segments?

How often do they run their ads?

How often do they change their ads (except for special events such as sales, introductory offers, and so

* A wide product line has lots of categories. A deep product line has a different appeal: few categories but great representation of choices within those categories. WalMart has a very wide product line. Woodworkers Warehouse has a very deep product line.

forth)? Do they change them because they don't work—or because (more likely) they are bored with seeing their message again and again?

What media do they use? What specific papers, magazines, radio or television, or other media?

If they use direct mail, collect the mailings to see what works (they'll keep doing it) and what doesn't (it'll be discontinued). What can you learn from these packages?

Red alert! Here are some common danger signs to look out for. Is your competitor:

- Building a new warehouse?
- Purchasing additional property?
- Developing a new image?
- Changing their positioning?
- Changing price strategies?
- Spiffing up their premises, inside and out?
- Increasing delivery capacity?
- Stepping up advertising frequency?
- Adding salespeople?
- Expanding their trading area?
- Using the Internet to reach new markets or better service old markets?
- Using the Internet to provide detailed product information?
- Adding services?
- Lengthening business hours?
- Redesigning products?
- Conducting professional market research?

Is your own business:

- Losing customers?
- Losing market share?
- Losing sales volume?
- Experiencing cash flow problems?
- Suffering relatively high employee turnover?
- Always playing "follow the leader"—with your competitor setting the pace?

Out of this nettle danger we pluck this flower safety.
WILLIAM SHAKESPEARE

Do not use low price as your competitive edge. You cannot afford to do this.

Do not use low price to enter a market. You will be perceived as offering less value than your competitors.

Do not use low price to differentiate yourself from your competitors. They'll laugh as you slowly drown in red ink.

Although Chapter 8 is devoted to pricing, we want you to realize that small businesses simply cannot afford to compete on price. Your pockets are not deep enough to compete with the giants. How should you compete with WalMart or Amazon.com? Not on price! Anything but price!

Unless, that is, your business objective is Chapter 11 reorganization (if you are lucky).

One way to learn a lot about your competitors is to visit their Web sites. How can you find them?

Starbucks hopes to extend its brand by moving on to sandwiches, salads, and more. The company is testing $5.50 sandwiches at its Washington, D.C., coffee shops and is cooking breakfast, lunch and dinner at Cafe Starbucks restaurants in Seattle, which have liquor licenses and offer table service. Although Starbucks is having a hard time meeting customers' high expectations, if it can develop a viable food menu for its 2,000 coffee bars, it is in a position to become an instant force in fast food. Starbucks claims it serves eight million customers a week, who typically make 18 visits a month to its coffee shops. (*The Wall Street Journal*, March 16, 1999, B-1)

Andy found a place for our editor Jere Calmes to order hard tack, an inedible form of Civil War cracker, by visiting *www.infoseek.com* and entering "hardtack" as the question. The source came up right away. Elapsed time: less than three minutes. Strangely enough, searching by *www.ask.com* (Ask Jeeves) and *www.webcrawler.com* turned up plenty of references to hard tack, mainly recipes, but no source. There is a lesson here: Try more than one search engine since each one operates just slightly differently.

If your competitors are serious about the Internet, they'll publicize their Web site address everywhere—in their print ads, business cards, trade publications, radio and television ads. Everywhere.

To find indirect competitors' sites, use a search engine such as *www.infoseek.com* and search by key words (also called "metatags"), which lead people to these sites. If you aren't used to using a search engine, learn. It's easy. You'll quickly pick up search techniques by trying, failing, trying again.

Visit as many competitive Web sites as you feel necessary. Most are linked to similar sites that will be closely related. Save the sites you want to revisit in a separate "favorites" file (available in almost every server) and revisit them once a week.

The Internet is such a dynamic marketplace that you can't afford to just check it out once in a while. Daily visits may be too much, but weekly visits will probably be needed to keep you up to date.

You can't always get what you want
But if you try sometimes
You just might find
You get what you need.

MICK JAGGER

7

What Do Your Customers Want from You?

Who buys what—and where, when, and why—are key pieces of marketing information. By figuring out the answers to the following questions, you can be more customer focused, and therefore more successful, than your competition.

For each product, product line, or service you offer, determine:

- Who makes the buying decision?
- What's the size of the sale in dollars?
- How many units are sold?
- What's your cost per sale?
- What do your customers buy?
- When do they buy?
- Are their purchases seasonal?
- Why do they buy your product or service?
- Where do they make the buying decision?
- How do they finance their purchase?
- How do your customers view your products or services?

Keep in mind that customers buy solutions to their problems, and satisfaction of their wants and needs. They buy benefits of a product or service—the "what's in it for me"—rather than its features. A feature (a

Database marketing has allowed supermarkets to home in on various segments of their market by tracking consumers' purchases and behavior. In some cases, the information is so detailed that the supermarket knows which combination of products were made in each purchase. Who knows—it may even be possible to anticipate a consumer's needs and make a direct approach with a solution for those needs. (Jim Blythe, *The Essence of Consumer Behavior*, London: Prentice Hall, 1997, page 154)

cotton/polyester-blend fabric) is something you or your product development person get excited about. A benefit (it doesn't have to be ironed) is something that excites your customer.

Other examples: Consumers don't go to a hardware store looking for a 1/4-inch drill bit—what they need is a 1/4-inch hole. Calvin Klein isn't selling perfume. He's selling sex. Coca-Cola isn't just selling a beverage that's sweet and quenches thirst. It provides "the pause that refreshes."

Know what excites your customers. Provide them with solutions to their problems. Give them something that makes them happy and their lives easier.

In the factory we make cosmetics.
In the store we sell hope.

CHARLES REVSON

How can you make your customers happy? Look at your products and services from their point of view and project that perspective in your marketing efforts.

This is what helped make WalMart's founder, Sam Walton, the largest retailer in the United States. Walton said he acted as "agent" for his customers. He'd find out what his customers wanted to buy and then go to manufacturers and wholesalers and buy the products on his customers' behalf.

Remember: Customers will not buy a product that does not meet their needs; nor will they buy junk. To be successful, you must be as focused on their needs as they are.

The art of showmanship is to give the public what it wants just before it knows what it wants.

DAVID BELASCO

How do you find out what your customers want and need? By doing market research. There is no substitute for hard facts and solid information about your market.

The first step is figuring out what kind of information you're looking for. For example, do you have a hunch that there's a great market for product X, but you're not sure who will buy it? Are you trying to tap new markets to find more customers for product X? Are you trying to figure out why sales of product X have not met your projections? Is demand for product X waning, and do you think that product Y would be more appropriate? Do you think product X isn't being distributed as widely as it should? Is your market aware of product X and what it does? Is your advertising resulting in what you'd hoped it would?

The list is endless. Get out your notebook and make a list of market-research questions you want answered.

What we see depends mainly on what we look for.

JOHN LUBBOCK

Next figure out how you'll get the information you need and how much it will cost. Is this information at your fingertips? Is it something you can generate in a few hours' work, or from making 10 or 15 phone

One company thinks it's found a way to cluster consumers based on how they shop and spend money. In 1999, Transactional Data Solutions (TDS), a joint venture between MasterCard International and Symmetrical Resources, issued its first National Merchant Advisor Report, which covers consumer buying habits in more than 30 categories, including department stores, apparel, catalogers, and travel. TDS can also identify, among other factors, which clusters visit the merchant most and spend the most, the extent to which the retailer "shares" consumers with competitors and the composition of new and repeat customer segments. Using TDS reports, clients can pinpoint which media index high with particular groups and then focus their advertising in those particular outlets. (*American Demographics*, April 1999)

In the mid-1970s, Gerber Products Company heeded rosy sales forecasts and introduced a new cereal for infants. When sales failed to take off, managers became perplexed. To figure out what was going on, they began looking for answers in-house. Company information on the cereal's distribution revealed that it was being distributed through only 25 percent of the outlets originally planned for. (Roger A. Kerin and Robert A. Peterson, *Strategic Marketing Problems*, Englewood Cliffs: Prentice Hall, 1995, page 115)

calls? Or will you need a staffer's help? Can you take an informal survey of your customers by placing a suggestion box in your store or office? Can you include a survey in your next mailing? Should you set up a telephone bank and hire temporary help? Does the kind of research you need to do call for skills and resources you don't have, and would it be best to hire market research professionals to get the information you need?

Sometimes things are simpler than we think. Sometimes they're a lot more complicated. If you're not sure how to proceed in your quest for market research, get a professional's opinion. A professor or grad student at your university's business school can help, as can an ad agency.

To open a shop is easy, to keep it open is an art.

CONFUCIUS

Make sure the information you get is accurate, timely, and relevant to your needs. Bad information begets bad decision making, which can result in an early demise for your product or service.

There are three kinds of lies: lies,
damned lies and statistics.

MARK TWAIN

Take advantage of all the information that's available to you at no cost. Start in-house, with your own sales records and any databases you may have on your customers. Talk to everyone in your company who has contact with customers—salespeople, office assistants, customer service representatives, delivery people, and so on. Find out what's on your customers' minds, what they're asking about, what (if anything) they're unhappy about, and what they think about your products or services.

These kinds of informal "discussions" often yield valuable information and should be a regular and ongoing part of your inexpensive market research efforts. Your staff is your company's most valuable resource—never overlook what they have to say.

A well-informed employee is the best salesperson a company can have.

E. J. THOMAS

Your suppliers are a mother lode of information for what's going on in your industry and with your competitors. Chances are that they'll be even more inclined to talk with you if you pay your bills on time and send new customers their way.

Reference librarians are another great resource. They can cheerfully direct you to books, publications, Web sites, and trade associations appropriate for your type of business.

Wisdom is better than rubies.

PROVERBS 8:11

When it comes to market research gone awry, there are two classic examples. First is the 1958 Ford Edsel, introduced in September 1957. Although millions of dollars had been spent, market research for the Edsel had come to a screeching halt several years earlier—a time when consumers' preferences were changing. To make matters worse, a recession was in high gear and demand for cars was decelerating. (Robert F. Hartley, *Marketing Mistakes*, New York: John Wiley & Sons, 1992, pages 156–157)

The second was when Coca-Cola changed the taste of its flagship brand in 1986. Although company research focused heavily on blind taste tests, participants were not told that the Coke they'd grown to love would be replaced with the new formula. Loyal customers were furious, and Coca-Cola brought back its "Classic" formula in time to avoid a complete fiasco. (Robert M. McMath, *What Were They Thinking?* New York: Times Books, 1998, page 124)

> Before building the prototype for its 21st-century look, Burger King asked what customers wanted in the ideal fast-food place. "A stress-free experience" was their response, according to Jacqueline McCook, company head of strategic planning. Patrons had complained about hard-to-read menu boards, crowded eating areas and tables bolted to the floor. Their overall impression of the chain? Boring, but they love the food. If the environment were more pleasant, they'd come more often. (*The Wall Street Journal*, April 14, 1999, B-1)

The best way to learn more about your customers is to go directly to them. The more information you have about them, the better you'll be able to serve them. There are several ways to accomplish this.

One is to visit them in their homes or offices, to see how they use your product or service. Japanese research often works this way. One appliance manufacturer there took 200 photos of actual Japanese kitchens and concluded that manufacturers had to address the shortage of space when designing appliances. Herb Kelliher, CEO of Southwest Airlines, gets feedback from his customers by handing out tickets and checking bags.

Listen to your customers. You'll learn a lot.

There is no royal road to learning.

GREEK PROVERB

Another way to get information from your customers is to ask for it. Did you ever notice that whenever you buy a hair dryer, electric shaver, a piece of luggage, or any other small household appliance, there's a brief questionnaire enclosed? Believe it or not, many of these are actually filled out and returned to manufacturers. As long as they can remain anonymous, customers don't mind answering a few questions.

Small businesses can use surveys and questionnaires to learn a lot about their customers. In general, the more brief your survey (six to eight questions), the more likely your customers are to fill it out and return it.

Hand our your survey when you give your customer his or her receipt. Offer an incentive (10 percent off on your next purchase!) to get people to respond. You could even pose questions online, on your Web site or in a chat room. Participating in a chat on the Internet is a great way to get instant feedback, provided you're in the right chat room with the right people.

Ask, and it shall be given you; seek, and ye shall find; knock, and it shall be opened unto you.

ST. MATTHEW

In addition to whatever marketing questions you want answered, also ask your customers and prospects what newspapers and magazines they read. That way, you can determine the best places to run your ads. Ask their age and gender, if demographics are relevant to your marketing efforts. Ask whom they consider the competition, so you'll know whom you're up against. Ask if they use the Internet, what radio stations they listen to, and what TV shows they watch so you can find the best way to reach them. Ask their name and address on occasion, knowing that this sacrifice of anonymity will result in fewer returns but in more detailed information that will help you build a prospect list.

Answers to these questions can help you learn who your prospective customers are, how to appeal to them, which media to use to reach them, what to emphasize in your advertising, whom they consider your competition, and what they want out of a product like yours.

When Roger Hewson began Sabre Yachts, he reckoned that the potential customers might just have a few ideas of their own that could be accommodated safely in his proposed range of sailboats. He armed a few employees with Polaroid cameras, clipboards, and pencils and sent them off to boat shows. Their mission: Elicit comments from people at the shows about what they liked, disliked, wanted to change or improve on the competitors' boat; then capture that information, along with the names and addresses of those people. Like that galley layout? Snap—and the comments went right on the back of the photo. Don't like the way the seat in the cockpit feels? Snap. More data entered. Armed with hundreds of these photos and comments, the designers produced boats that immediately captured a sizable chunk of the market. Of course, the built-in prospect file didn't hurt. Wouldn't you be flattered if a manufacturer sent you a brochure that thanked you for your input?

Tracking service requests helped the downtown Chicago Marriott hotel discover that two-thirds of its guest calls to housekeeping were for an iron and ironing board. So instead of replacing the black-and-white TVs in the bathrooms of concierge-level guest rooms (housekeeping had received no calls requesting color TVs in the bathroom), the hotel spent $20,000 putting irons and ironing boards in all the guest rooms. (Peter R. Dickson, *Marketing Management*, Fort Worth: The Dryden Press, 1994, page 564)

Update your survey when necessary, and repeat the process regularly. Things about your customers, prospects, and market are always changing, and you need up-to-date information in order to stay ahead of your competitors.

Focus groups are another helpful research tool. They're typically comprised of 6 to 12 people who participate in a two-hour discussion about a particular subject, and are most useful for getting feedback on new products, product usage, and consumer shopping behavior. Sometimes participants are paid. Sometimes lunch is all that's needed.

Focus groups work best when they're made up of consumers with similarities regarding age, income, education, interests, and values. A knowledgeable discussion leader can prevent one or two vocal individuals from dominating the group by going around the table early on in the discussion and encouraging everyone to participate.

Customer, distributor, or franchisee advisory councils are permanent focus groups that regularly come together to provide feedback on what's happening in the market. They're used most often in business-to-business marketing.

Giant corporations use test markets to try out a new product on a smaller scale before introducing it nationwide. Movie studios spend several hundreds of thousands of dollars on test screenings and audience research before a new film is released. Why? Because the cost of a flop in some markets is measured in millions, not hundreds of thousands, of dollars.

It is not the crook in modern business that we fear, but the honest man who doesn't know what he is doing.

OWEN D. YOUNG

Trade shows are great places to gather information on products and services that other companies are introducing to customers and distributors. Not only do you get to see just what these products and services are—you get to see just how interested customers and distributors are in buying them! And if that's not the cat's meow, you also get to network with your competitors' salespeople to find out what's happening with them and other rivals. Those opportunities are more than worth the price of admission!

Personal relations are the important thing for ever and ever.

E. M. FORSTER

Don't overlook other business owners as valuable information resources. Talk with fellow business owners in your industry who are in noncompeting areas. Chances are that if you tell them about a marketing strategy that worked for you, they'll tell you about what worked for them—and maybe lots more. Everyone benefits by talking with others in similar businesses.

Relationships with other business owners in your community are also worth cultivating. Not only do

A 90 percent failure rate for new products, along with fierce competition for market share, has prompted many companies to get into stores and talk with consumers as they reach for products on the shelf. Manufacturers want to know why people buy its brand, or that of the competition. Is it price? Packaging? Promotional displays? A crisp $5 bill is offered to shoppers who agree to answer a few questions. A 1998 study by Frito Lay found that the average shopper spends only 21 minutes buying groceries and covers only 23 percent of the store. People with shopping lists don't necessarily stick to them and 59 percent of all supermarket purchases are unplanned. (*American Demographics*, April 1999)

Know how to ask questions. A study conducted by Xerox learning systems established that successful salespeople use words such as *what, where, why, how,* and *tell me,* which allow the customer to respond more freely. Such questions are called open probes. Closed probes, using words such as *is, do, have,* and *which* will limit answers to yes or no or a choice of alternatives. They do not get to the reasons behind the answers. (Peter R. Dickson, *Marketing Management,* Fort Worth: The Dryden Press, 1994, page 383)

you get a better understanding of what's going on in your community, but you also get an opportunity to make yourself and your business known to other decision makers. You never know where the next word-of-mouth referral is going to come from.

SECTION 3:

Growing Your Customer Base

8 How Do You Price Your Products and Services?

Pricing is a headache for every small business owner. There are few guidelines: what the traffic will bear, what the competitors are charging, some rules of thumb. Since pricing is such an important part of marketing—some say the most important—it makes sense for you to spend a lot of thought and research on setting the right prices for your products, in your markets, in your competitive environment.

How do you currently set prices? Chances are that you don't follow a conscious pricing strategy, one based on your customers' perception of value and your cost and profit structures.

Don't feel badly if your strategy isn't so rational. Few business owners set prices strategically; most either follow what everyone else is doing or (foolishly) try to compete on price. This presents you with a major opportunity to differentiate your business from those of your competitors and make more money.

You start by gathering four pieces of information. First, what do your customers perceive to be value in your kind of business? This calls for serious market research. Don't try to guess what they think and feel. You want to base your pricing on perceived value—that is, sell value not price.

Second, what is your cost structure? This includes all costs: overhead, promotion, storage and carrying charges, and financing costs, as well as the cost of the actual product. Your accountant can help you with this.

Stonewall Kitchens, a firm that makes and sells jams, salad dressings and barbecue sauces, recently thought about relocating 15 miles away from its York, Maine, headquarters to New Hampshire. "We really like being 'Made in Maine,'" explained co-founder Jim Stott. "Maine has better marketing panache than New Hampshire." Stonewall's customers, who pay $6.50 for a jar of jam, need to believe the company's food is special. To Mr. Stott, "Made in Maine" connotes attention to detail, pride of workmanship, and hard-working people. Most of the credit for that image goes to L.L. Bean, the Freeport, Maine, company that has been selling clothes and other mail-order items since 1912. (*The Wall Street Journal*, June 30, 1999, NE-1)

Third, what are your profit objectives? We like to say that profit is a fixed cost, just as important as rent or advertising. You aren't in business to break even.

And fourth, what is the competition up to? Your aim is to lead the pack, not follow it, but that does not imply that your pricing should be completely independent of your competitors'.

Once you have this information, you can start to set price ranges.

What is a cynic? A man who knows the price of everything and the value of nothing.

OSCAR WILDE

Prices are not rigid. The "right" price for your goods and services will float somewhere between a price ceiling ("what the traffic will bear") and a price floor (high enough to cover your cost and profit needs). It depends on your market to a very high degree. A hamburger at Lutéce will cost you $75, whereas a burger that is just as tasty will set you back $6 at Hamburger Hamlet. (This, by the way, is a good example of how customers perceive value.)

To find the price ceiling, look around. Comparison shop. Check out catalogs, price lists, quotes. Look at trade publications—they sometimes run pricing studies to help their members wrestle with thorny pricing issues.

The floor, your cost and profit structure, will change over time. Don't price below this floor unless you have a very good reason. Have stale inventory? Sell it for whatever you can get.

Elasticity, the technical study of the influence of price changes on the purchasing behavior of specific market segments, divides products into two categories. Elastic products are price sensitive. A small change in the price will result in significant shifts in unit sales. An inelastic product is insensitive to price changes (within reason!). At the very least you have to know the elasticity of your products. This once again calls for market research: How price sensitive are your core markets? Can you raise prices without losing market share? Or will a lower price gain market share while maintaining profitability since the higher unit sales will balance the slightly lower profit per unit?

Remember that revenue = price × unit sales. Whether your goal is to maximize revenue or maximize profit, you must keep this in mind. And above all, you must know what your markets are willing to pay for the value you provide them.

The real price of everything, what everything
really costs to the man who wants to acquire it,
is the toil and trouble of acquiring it.

ADAM SMITH

Full-cost pricing, linked with knowledge of your market segment and the competition, can provide a quick pricing method. But don't rely on this or any other mechanical pricing method alone. A flexible approach will serve you far better.

This works best if you can identify all of your operating costs and distribute them over your merchandise costs. You then add profit contribution to the

A study on the effects of price on the shopping public revealed that higher-income consumers are more likely to take advantage of bargain prices on certain products by stocking up, and by buying less of these goods when prices rise. It also shows that shoppers can be "trained" to buy on promotion. Aging baby boomers are thinking about retirement and trying to save money, not spend it. "It's now considered chic to save," said Kurt Barnard, president of *Barnard's Retail Trend Report*, a trends and consumer spending forecasting firm. Target, K-mart and other discount department stores have become popular among upper-income shoppers, and the discount department store industry is racking up annual sales of more than $310 billion. (*American Demographics*, "Those with More Buy for Less," April 1999)

augmented merchandise costs, divide by the number of units of merchandise, and lo! you have your unit prices.

If you sell all of your merchandise in the time frame allotted, this works pretty well. It is more useful as a way to narrow the price ranges you set earlier. If your merchandise doesn't sell, or if your operating costs change, you'll have to rethink this method.

Thinking of raising your prices? This works best if:

- Your market is growing commercial customers
- Your customers can build your price into their selling price
- Your product helps them make more money
- You have an image as the leader in service, reliability, quality, and product knowledge
- Your selling price is a tiny fraction of the customer's total costs

Price ceilings are seldom challenged—except by the market leader. Becoming the market leader isn't a bad aim and should be your primary marketing objective.

Don't follow leaders
Watch the parkin' meters.

BOB DYLAN

Here's a handy formula to keep in mind when setting prices:

Price = Image + Service + Product + Overhead + Risk + Profit

All these factors affect price. Pricing is inherently strategic and always involves competition. Your image can be high-end (Tiffany), low-end (K-Mart), or somewhere in between. High-end markets tend to be inelastic, providing wider margins than are possible in more cost-conscious segments. The tradeoff is that this high-end segment is relatively small and very hotly pursued.

At the other end of the spectrum are businesses that compete mainly on price, the category busters like Staples and Office Max and the big discounters. Their image tends to be businesslike, professional but certainly not fancy. Their market segment is huge but very elastic, ready to go elsewhere for a lower price.

Overhead costs also vary. High-end businesses pay high rent and high salaries for skilled sales staff, whereas low-end facilities tend to be warehouselike and relatively inexpensive, with low-paid sales staff. Once more, this is a tradeoff.

Both ends face risks. Tiffany worries about the costs of inventory and fluctuations in the economy. The stock market drops? So do Tiffany sales. Category busters and discounters face severe competition and also have to carry very large inventories. There's plenty of risk to go around.

Finally, both ends are profit driven. They just take different paths to their profit goals.

It is not that pearls fetch a high price because *men have dived for them: but on the contrary, men dive for them because they fetch a high price.*

RICHARD WHATELY

Coca-Cola's sales fell in the first quarter of 1999, a sharp downswing from the one to two-percent rise that Wall Street had expected. Coke officials attribute the slowdown to its efforts to push through its first price hike in five years—hikes that PepsiCo didn't match in many markets. (*Business Week*, April 2, 1999)

The cost of a cup of Starbucks coffee increased by a dime in May 1999, the first price hike in two years. Starbucks, whose coffee already is among the priciest, cited higher labor and space costs for the increase at its 2,000 coffee shops across North America. While a large coffee can cost as much as $2.50, an analyst at Alex Brown called demand for a cup of Starbucks coffee "fairly inelastic" to cost. (*The Wall Street Journal*, May 12, 1999, B-8)

Price/quality grids, like the one shown here, help locate market gaps. The same technique can be applied to your business. Where do you fit? Where do your competitors fit? This isn't brain surgery—it is a subjective look at the market.

You can use price/service, price/depth, price/specialty, quality/service, and as many other grids as your ingenuity can provide. Look for gaps, areas of the grids that are relatively empty. These can represent untapped opportunities.

Market researchers occasionally use these grids when interviewing market segments. How do your markets perceive your position on, say, the price/quality grid? Would this information help you? You can bet on it.

When people expect something for nothing,
they are sure to be cheated.

P. T. BARNUM

At the end of the day, the way your customers perceive value drives your pricing decisions. From their point of view, how do your products and services differ from the competing products and services? Note that this is from your customers' point of view, not yours.

Hint: The great "WIIFM?" is always present in your markets' thoughts. "WIIFM?" stands for "What's in it for me?" Perceived quality, perceived service, perceived value. All from the customer's point of view.

When I sell liquor, it's called bootlegging.
When my patrons serve it on silver trays on Lake Shore Drive, it's called hospitality.

AL CAPONE

Life insurance agents are experts at upgrading their customer and prospect bases. They deliberately trade up in order to overcome the price barriers involved in selling life insurance. Part of this is a function of aging. As the agent grows older, so will the clientele, and with age—maybe—their incomes will grow. Part of it, the part that separates successful agents from the less successful, is careful targeting of more affluent folks or more sizable businesses.

This takes courage. That may be why only a small fraction of insurance agents do it.

Why not try to trade up in your business? Can you choose to serve a wealthier market segment? The rewards are compelling: less price sensitivity, greater profits, even less competition.

The Yugo, a product of Yugoslavia, was introduced in the U.S. market in 1985 with what seemed a significant differential advantage: It was the lowest-priced car available in America. Unfortunately, a low price, if effective in winning customers, can be easily matched or countered by competitors. In Yugo's case, while it stubbornly maintained the lowest price, it had a growing number of competitors, both foreign and domestic, entering the market with cars that were of better quality, technologically superior and priced only modestly more than the Yugo. (Robert F. Hartley, *Marketing Mistakes*, New York: John Wiley & Sons, 1992, page 118)

Some independently owned funeral homes have stopped buying caskets from Hillenbrand Industries Inc., the number-one maker, through its Batesville Casket Company unit, angry over an agreement by Hillenbrand to sell caskets at lower prices to the nation's biggest funeral-home chain, Service Corp. International, Inc. Charles Anderson, owner of two funeral homes in Franklin, Ohio, stopped buying Hillenbrand caskets and is instead buying from Aurora Casket Company in Indiana. "They're sympathetic to independent funeral homes," he said. (*The Wall Street Journal*, February 23, 1999, A-8)

Be not afraid of growing slowly;
be afraid only of standing still.
CHINESE PROVERB

Here's a smattering of pricing strategies.

High volume, low price. This used to be called the Woolworth strategy but nowadays WalMart and its imitators are a better example.

Low volume, high price. Think Tiffany, Rolls Royce, Rodeo Drive.

Specialty. The more specialized your wares, the better your chances of charging higher prices. Look at the collectibles market. You got how much for that baseball card? You must be kidding!

Follow the leader. This is the most popular strategy. It is among the least effective.

Guess, or pricing on whim. Another popular but ineffective method. However, in some fields, it seems to work, especially in art and craft markets, where nobody really knows how to set prices.

Cost plus. Add on profit and overhead.

Mark-up and mark-on. These involve adding a set percentage of the merchandise cost to arrive at the desired profit per unit. Doubling is a popular approach: add 100 percent of merchandise cost and pray. Advertising agencies add a mark-up of 17.65 percent to all outsourced services like printing to arrive at a 15 percent gross margin on these services. This covers the often overlooked transaction costs such as negotiating with the printer.

Different markets, different price. Upstart, Andy's publishing company, had a sliding scale for banks of different sizes. Bigger banks paid higher rates for essentially the same level of service. He now has two day rates for his consulting work, one for nonprofits and one for regular businesses. Andi has two types of editorial rates, one for nonprofits and one for corporate clients.

MSRP or manufacturer's suggested retail price. Why would the manufacturer know your markets and cost structures better than you do?

Image and status pricing. A restaurant with an image of elegance and high status will charge more than a roadside diner. Unless, that is, the roadside diner shares that image.

Artists and craftspersons face an especially tough pricing problem. If their works are displayed in a gallery or similar venue, then the gallery owner will draw on his or her knowledge of the market to set prices. Ditto with stores—Andi sells her pottery in several gift shops, which makes her pricing decisions easier.

For artists and craftspersons who aren't fortunate enough to establish a good relation with a gallery or store, the common advice has been to haggle: Set a high-ish price, then be prepared to change that price to accommodate the customer. This will usually yield a price range that over time will rise (assuming that the artist's reputation and output grow).

This is a classic value-driven market. The customer's perception of value is far more important than the artist's—but that perception can be changed. A gallery sells aesthetic judgment (a great benefit) as well as artwork, and that benefit adds considerable value.

Mercedes Benz is reviving the Maybach, a 1930s luxury brand that stretches 19 feet and could go for $350,000. Mercedes hopes to sell up to 2,000 of them, mostly in the U.S., starting in 2003. "The Rolls-Royce is an old car," sniffs a Mercedes spokesman. "We are betting that people will want to buy the same kind of luxury with modern technology." (*Forbes*, May 17, 1999, page 98)

Everything in Rome has its price.

JUVENAL

Pricing consulting services is a bit simpler than pricing art. There are several basic billing methods ranging from hourly rates to day rates to project rates, each of which has benefits and drawbacks. They all reflect the same pricing logic, though, and differ mainly in how well they meet the markets' needs.

Our favorite method goes like this.

Step 1: Decide what you need or wish to make annually. Each year has 2,000 business hours (50 weeks at 40 hours per week = 2,000 hours).

Step 2: Figure the hourly rate *without* overhead.

Step 3: Figure the annual overhead costs, including your SEP-IRA contributions, marketing costs, rent, insurances, and so on. Don't forget that profit is a fixed cost and that you have to be paid both as a consultant and as a business owner. Now *double* this figure.

Step 4: Divide this number by 2,000 to get an hourly overhead burden rate. You double this figure because your time spent marketing and performing administrative tasks has to be paid for one way or another. Not all hours are billable hours.

Step 5: Add this to the hourly rate of Step 2. This yields your hourly billing rate.

Suppose you need $60,000 a year to pay your children's tuition and cover your own expenses, and have $45,000 per year in overhead costs.

1. $60,000
2. $60,000 ÷ 2,000 = $30/hour
3. $45,000 × 2 = $90,000
4. $90,000 ÷ 2,000 = $45/hour
5. $30 + $45 = $75/hour

Howard Shenson, a consultant to consultants, figures out pricing this way.

Step 1: Establish a daily rate, the cost of your time.
Step 2: Calculate your monthly overhead.
Step 3: Calculate your overhead rate, which equals total overhead divided by number of billable hours per month.
Step 4: Profit equals 16 to 24 percent of your daily labor plus overhead rate.
Step 5: Round up the total to the nearest $25 to arrive at your day rate.

Using the same assumptions as in the preceding example: $60,000 desired income, $45,000 annual overhead. Assume 15 billable days per month.

1. $60,000 ÷ 250 = $240/day
2. $45,000 ÷ 12 + $3,750/month
3. $3,750 ÷ 15 billable days per month = $250
4. Profit = 20% ($240 + $250) = $98
5. Day rate = $240 + 250 + 98 = $588; round this up to $600/day
6. $600 ÷ 8 = $75/hour

With WalMart's $10 billion cash offer to buy Asda Group PLC, Britain's third-largest food retailer, shopping for the British may never be the same. With its low-pricing policies and customer-friendly attitude, Wal-Mart is likely to change the face of British retailing and its reputation for high prices and surly service. Now retailers will be looking at how to improve value and at routes of consolidation to protect their future. (*The Wall Street Journal*, July 16, 1999, A-23)

Incidentally, many experts advise against billing on an hourly rate, fearing that this leads to treating your services as a commodity and getting you enmeshed in unprofitable discussions about how many hours did you really need to provide the service. Your choice: Look for a project rate or bill in smaller segments.

Hassled by price competition? Here are 10 ways to fight back.

Personalize your business. Small businesses can become extensions of the owner's persona, and this is more appealing to a substantial portion of the market than an artificial "Have a nice day!" from a paid greeter.

Specialize. As noted before, specialty connotes higher price. At the Farmer's Market in Portsmouth, you may pay more for a lamb chop than at the supermarket, but you'll be dealing with a farmer who specializes in raising organically fed sheep.

Provide better financing than the competition. Small stores sometimes extend limited credit to their clients, a convenience that adds value. A community store where children can buy a half gallon of milk to be paid for by their parents the next day will get a lot of business from the neighborhood for a low cost.

Provide more convenience through longer hours, or hours more suited to your customers than the big guys provide.

Use superior demonstrations. Our friend Bert Myer went to a big box store looking for a new computer. The clerk had no idea how to configure the computer and tried to fake it. Bert went to a smaller store, one with more knowledgeable staff, where his needs were met.

Improve your communications with your markets. They may not realize what you can do—keep them informed.

Change your market niche.

Raise your prices and sell on value, not price.

Provide superior service. Andy buys radios, televisions, and VCRs from Tony's Radio & TV, a small but very service-oriented store in Portsmouth, New Hampshire. He pays more but makes up for it with the service they provide when his grandchildren insert popsicles into the VCR.

Provide higher-quality products. The big box stores don't purvey state-of-the-art devices, nor the most expensive, highest quality. They aim for a mass market, not the niche that buys on quality.

The idea is to sidestep price competition and fight on value. You'll lose the low-ball customers but you'd lose them anyway. Someone will always provide cheaper, shoddier, lower-cost products than you can. Or would want to.

Most of the change we think we see in life
Is due to truths being in and out of favor.
Robert Frost, "The Black Cottage"

Sometimes you can allay customers' price sensitivity by providing:

- Credits
- Rebates
- Discounts
- Generous return policies

Before the spring of 1999, "gelly pens" were just a pricier version of a ballpoint pen that was supposed to be used for arts and crafts. Then, all of a sudden, huge numbers of U.S. kids between ages four and 14 decided they had to have a Milky Gel Roller, the gelly pen made by Pentel Company of Tokyo. Once kids discovered the Milky's snappy phosphorescent colors, they began turning their hands, arms, ankles and even cheeks into easels. A pricy crafts pen had been transformed into a cheap toy. (*The Wall Street Journal*, June 15, 1999, A-1)

Amazon.com's 50 percent discounts on best-selling books is touching off a price war in one of the Internet's most fiercely contested markets. To some extent, Amazon may be able to treat best-selling books as loss leaders that attract customers into its on-line store where they can be tempted by other merchandise that isn't priced so cheaply. Amazon's share of best-sellers as a percent of total sales is slightly lower than the 10 to 25 percent share at traditional bookstores, and Amazon's customers often buy computer books or older titles. (*The Wall Street Journal*, May 17, 1999, B-11)

- Free shipping and handling
- Loss leaders
- Senior citizen's discounts
- Student discounts

You may have noticed that a number of major direct marketers now offer their own VISAs or MasterCards. L.L. Bean, for example, offers free shipping and monogramming to their credit card customers, as well as a rebate based on use of the cards for other purchases. This very effectively negates price competition, builds customer loyalty, and makes the customer feel pretty special. They also offer the best return policy in their industry.

Whenever you see a successful business,
someone once made a courageous decision.

PETER DRUCKER

---

9 How Do You Promote Your Products and Services?

Promotion includes all the ways you communicate with your markets to make them aware of your products and services. Advertising and public relations are promotional tools, as are special events, newsletters, news releases, public speaking, word of mouth, feature stories, networking, and lots more!

The first step in any promotional campaign is deciding which image and message you want to convey, and then determining the right promotional tool or combination of tools to use. Your challenge is to make your promotional message stand out from the hundreds of others that compete for your market's attention every day. As a result, your promotion has to make an impact—it has to say something, and say it well and quickly. It has to make a favorable impression and spur people to take the action(s) you want them to.

Depending on the nature of your business and your skills, you may feel comfortable doing some of your own promotion. But unless advertising or public relations is your profession, you're better served having someone else write your ads or newsletter, produce your annual report, or organize your special event. Surely you've heard the expression that a lawyer who represents himself or herself has a fool for a client?

Despite their initial costs, professionals can put together a promotional campaign more quickly and more effectively than you can. Remember:

JCPenney killed Kenny, and the rest of the *South Park* gang. The Comedy Central show about foul-mouthed grade-school children has drawn criticism from conservative groups because of its language and violence. JCPenney has decided to stop ordering merchandise related to the popular animated show after getting some negative feedback from customers. (*The Concord Monitor*, April 29, 1999, D-16)

You can save them a lot of work, and yourself a lot of money, by providing them with market research on who your customers are and why they buy from you rather than the competition.

Although we could devote whole books each to promotion, advertising, and public relations (and we just might someday!), we're limited to only two chapters in this book. In this chapter, we'll focus on special promotions and public relations, and devote Chapter 10 solely to advertising.

All publicity is good,
except an obituary notice.

BRENDAN BEHAN

With all promotional efforts, remember that first impressions last and image always counts. You have just seven seconds to make a good first impression, according to Roger Ailes, former Republican strategist and now chairman and CEO of Fox News. How you combine words, graphics, color, style, sounds, photos, and video says thousands of words about what your business is and what you're trying to communicate.

For starters, think about the name of your business. Your business name can be one of your most effective and least expensive marketing tools. Does it say what you do? Does it speak to customers' needs? Make sure you avoid vague or misleading names, forgettable names, and names that are hard to pronounce or spell. Bad names: John Smith Enterprises, ABC Quality Services. Good names: Rent-a-Geek, Critter

Care (don't use the letter "k" because people won't find you in the phone book).

Then think about appearance. That's why major corporations spend thousands and thousands of dollars creating memorable logos and appropriate graphic looks for their companies. The style of the logo, the way a product looks, the way it's packaged, the quality of paper stock used for letterhead or brochures—these all communicate distinct messages about a product or service. A magazine printed on heavy, glossier paper stock with lots of beautiful photos and elegant typography, like *Architectural Digest* or *Saveur*, has more visual appeal than *The Economist* or *TV Guide*. Receiving a small gift box is always exciting for those of us who love jewelry, but imagine how much more thrilling it would be if that box were a small blue one from Tiffany's. Coffee beans in a plain brown bag from your local grocery store might taste as good as those from Starbucks, but might not be your choice for a gift basket.

> When it comes to beverages, people drink image. Think about Maxwell House coffee being "good to the last drop." Absolute vodka is "absolute elegance." Perrier is "earth's first soft drink." "Coke is it," except when New Coke was introduced in 1986—a marketing *faux pas* which implied that the Coke we loved was really not "it." (Robert McMath, *What Were They Thinking?* New York: Times Books, 1998, page 107)

Pleasing ware is half sold.

GEORGE HERBERT

How consistent is your company's promotional image? Take this easy test, first pointed out to us in 1983 at Andy's company, Upstart Publishing, by then graphic designer Joni Doherty. Gather all the printed materials your company uses for marketing purposes—business cards, letterhead, brochures, signage, advertisements, invoices, flyers, and so on. Place them side by side on a big table. Do they look like they're part of the same graphic family? Does your logo appear on every piece? Are your logo colors and paper stock always the same, or have some clear relationship? If you answer no to any of these questions, you've got a problem that demands immediate attention from a professional graphic designer!

If your employees wear uniforms, is there a "look" that customers will associate with your company? What impression do these uniforms give? Does the wearer look clean? Neat? Trendy? Professional? Even if your employees don't wear uniforms, per se, is there a look that tells customers who's serving whom? Think of the pervasive khaki pants and white shirts on Gap salespeople, or the gray Brooks Brothers suits you'd see in a downtown law firm.

If customers visit your place of business, what's the atmosphere like? Do staffers immediately give customers attention, or do they leave them alone for a while? How do customers feel? Attended to? In a hurry? Like browsing for hours? Comfortable asking questions?

How are customers treated when they call your business? Are employees friendly and helpful?

Make a list of 10 descriptions you'd like your company to have. Fun to work with? Able to meet deadlines? Professional? Compassionate? Great with kids? A leader in the community? A leader in the field? Creative? Can work wonders on a shoestring? Add this list to your notebook.

If Botticelli were alive today he'd be working for Vogue.

PETER USTINOV

Image is only part of your promotional efforts. But it's the part that tends to grab your target's attention first. After you've figured out what kind of image you want to project, focus on what you want to tell people. Effective promotional messages motivate your customers or prospects to take a certain action and promise them a benefit if they do.

For example, do you want to let customers know about a new product, a new service, a new location, or new hours of business? Do you want new customers in new locations to become aware of what you have to offer? Are there new uses of your product or service you want customers to know about? Do you want to educate prospective customers so they can make a more informed decision and thereby purchase your product? Do you want to let customers know that kids and pets are welcome at your place of business? That you're a friend of the environment?

Frankly, to manufacture thought
Is like a masterpiece by a weaver wrought.
JOHANN WOLFGANG VON GOETHE

Once you determine what you want to tell people, you need to figure out what's in it for them. Remember from Chapter 7 that people buy benefits, not features. People don't buy soap. They buy clean, soft skin. The corner store doesn't sell milk. It sells convenience. Which benefits fit the message you want to send to your targeted audience?

Whatever your message's content, make sure it's style is an attention-grabber. People don't buy a product just because you tell them to. Editors don't

The Pillsbury Doughboy has landed in India to pitch a product he has just about abandoned in America: plain old flour. But selling packaged flour in India is no easy task, because most Indian housewives still buy raw wheat in bulk, clean it themselves and take it to a neighborhood mill to grind it. To help reach those housewives, the Doughboy has gotten a makeover. In TV spots, he presses his palms together and bows in the traditional Indian greeting. He speaks six regional languages. (*The Wall Street Journal*, May 5, 1999, B-1)

Newsletters Plus was a fast-growing, successful 12-year-old, $10 million business whose 48 employees helped big companies craft their sales strategy and image. But owner Moira Shanahan saw a dull company name that didn't reflect the firm's expanding services. To reinvent the company, she worked with staff, focus groups and clients to come up with a new name, Braindance. Shanahan launched a series of direct mailings to 5,000 prospects, including some former clients, of postcards and boxes of logo-emblazoned promotional goods announcing the firm's relaunch. A sales manager from Sun Microsystems, who had hired Shanahan years earlier to do newsletters, called as soon as he received his box, because he had no idea her company did so many things. (*Business Week*, "How's This for a Change?" January 28, 1999)

read news releases just because they're on their desk. People don't attend special events just because they happen to be going on. They take action because there's something in it for them. The consumer buys Special K cereal because it's low-fat and nutritious. The editor sees a story that's of interest to his or her readers. People go to a book signing to meet an author, or to a benefit performance in order to support a favored charity.

Then tell your audience what you want them to do. Visit your showroom? Fill in and return a questionnaire? Use a coupon for their next purchase? Ask for a free sample? Make a phone call? Reserve tickets? Send for a brochure? Be precise and be clear.

Advertising which promises no benefit to the consumer does not sell, yet the majority of campaigns contain no promise whatever. (That is the most important sentence in this book. Read it again.)

David Ogilvy in Ogilvy on Advertising

There are lots of promotional tools you can use to get word out to your market. Using several at once often works best. For this book, we've divided them up into the categories of events, announcements, and partnerships.

Hosting a special event can be a great way to get your message out to a targeted group specifically invited to the event. The New Hampshire Writers' Project, a nonprofit group Andi works with that promotes the literary arts, hosts small dinner parties with well-known authors in order to entice well-heeled individuals to support the organization. A dress shop might host a fashion show, a hobby shop might sponsor craft demonstrations, a book store could provide a story time for young readers. The list is endless.

Sales are another event that's sure to bring customers into your shop. What hard-core shopper can resist signs reading "50% off!" "Lowest prices of the year!" and the just plain "SALE" in bright red letters?

Grand openings, reopenings, and open houses are other ways to increase traffic to your establishment. They help prospective customers satisfy their curiosity about your merchandise, and provide you with a forum to tell them why your product or service is superior to that of the competition. Free ice-cream cones and cookies encourage people to walk in the door, and raffles and door prizes can boost attendance even more.

The sign brings customers.
Jean de la Fontaine

Trade shows can also give you lots of promotional bang for your bucks. You can make contacts with prospective customers and suppliers, and check out the competition. In some specialized markets, attending the annual trade show is an absolute must.

You don't have to be an exhibitor to attend a trade show. But if you do have a booth, have a dish of candy and a specialty item with your name on it that people can take with them. Most important, have a way of collecting names and addresses of people who visit your booth. A drawing for a gift certificate or some

Nature's NorthWest health food chain licensed software to distribute custom-printed newsletters at its checkouts. When the cashier scans a frequent shopper card, the card's transaction history triggers a newsletter reflecting that consumer's purchase history and areas of interest (individuals check off interests on their application for the card). Bought herbal supplements and organic meat on your last visit? Interested in exercise? Your newsletter might have a schedule of local exercise classes, a recipe for meat and a coupon for more herbs. The newsletter prints at the checkout counter in seven seconds, faster than the cashier can make change and bag groceries. The store tracks which bar-coded coupons are redeemed from the newsletter, and then adjusts the shopper's newsletter accordingly the next time they make a purchase. (*American Demographics*, March 1999)

> Civic events allow businesses to gain wide exposure without spending a ton of money. Every June, Portsmouth, New Hampshire, where Andy lives, hosts Market Square Day, a day-long festival where merchants take their wares to outdoor booths lining the town's streets. Crafters and other retailers join them, and other businesses sponsor music and kids activities throughout the day. Foods of all sorts and music abound, and Market Square Day is a time to see and be seen!

other irresistible item will do the trick—all people have to do is leave their business card in a bowl on your table. That way, you have a record of who's visited your booth.

Remember that the sole purpose of trade shows is to establish new contacts, not to strike business deals on the spot. The key with trade show leads is to promptly follow up on them. Personalized follow-up letters should be sent and dated the day after the show's end. That's the time prospective customers and distributors judge the service of a company against the efforts of competitors.

To be persuasive, we must be believable.
To be believable, we must be credible.
To be credible, we must be truthful.

EDWARD R. MURROW

Promotional announcements about your product or service can take a variety of forms.

Flyers and posters work well if you're geographically segmenting your market and your distribution is limited. Flyers don't have to be works of art and can be economically reproduced at your local copy shop. Posters, on the other hand, require more attention to graphic design because of their staying power. If they're especially appealing, they can be framed and displayed for a long time. But like billboards, posters need to be strategically placed.

If it works for your business, print up a free resource list for customers, with your company's name, logo, address, and phone number prominently displayed on it. Or you could reprint an article that's relevant to your customers. A book store could have on hand for customers copies of *The New York Times* bestsellers list or a list of Web sites just for history buffs. A paint store could have a do and don't list for refinishing furniture. A lawyer might give you a list of 10 reasons to write a will.

Again, the list is endless for what you could do. Remember that anything you do to make your product or service "better" than that of your competitors gives your customers yet another reason to buy from you.

> *Beat your gong and sell your candies.*
> CHINESE PROVERB

Your local or regional newspaper can be an important promotional resource—provided your news is something that's of interest to its readers. Never try to pass off a news item for what's really an advertisement. If an editor detects even the faintest trace of commercial motives in your news release, off it will go to the circular file.

News releases are great ways to announce special events, classes, new management-level hires, and awards won. Just make sure your news release goes to the right person and meets his or her deadline. A rule of thumb is to get your release in the appropriate person's hands more than three weeks before you want to see it in print in a newspaper or hear it on air. Magazines require even more lead time. To be absolutely sure about the publication you're interested

Circle K launched a $100 million promotion in 1990 at its more than 3,700 convenience stores to communicate a change in store prices that provided customers with more value for their dollar. The promotion centered on a "We're Driving Down Prices" game, which included some 180 million instant-winner, scratch-off tickets distributed to customers who made purchases at Circle K stores. Customers could win merchandise discounts, theme-park discounts, and grand prizes like Jeep Wranglers and round-trip airline tickets. The program competed against an initiative launched by 7-Eleven earlier that year. (Roger A. Kerin and Robert A. Peterson, *Strategic Marketing Problems*, Englewood Cliffs: Prentice Hall, 1995, page 595)

in, call ahead to confirm deadlines. If you've never written a news release, consult a public relations textbook for the appropriate professional format. Or hire a freelancer to write it for you.

Letters to the editor are a great positioning tool, particularly if your opinion is being attacked or misrepresented by others. Just make sure your letter is well thought out, timely, and well written. If you're not comfortable with your writing skills, get help from someone who's comfortable with theirs.

Everybody's entitled to his own opinion but no man had a right to be wrong in his facts.

BERNARD M. BARUCH

There are several ways to position yourself as an "expert" in your field. If your writing skills are good, you can write articles for trade publications on your area of expertise. If you're knowledgeable but not a skilled writer, don't let that deter you—hire a freelancer. If you've got the gift of gab, offer to be a guest on a radio or cable TV talk show. Call or write the producer of the show you're interested in to make your pitch. If you have something to say that's of interest to the general public, consider a public service announcement (PSA) for either radio or television.

Public speaking is a great way to get known. Instead of just attending a conference, get on the program! Or contact your church, synagogue, or local civic club about speaking there. If public speaking is not your forte, get some coaching or training ahead of time. Toastmasters groups are great places to start. Call your local chamber of commerce or check listings in your local newspaper to see if one meets in your area.

If you have lots to say on an ongoing basis about what's going on in your field, write a column for a trade magazine or newspaper, or consider publishing a newsletter—either in print or online. Both columns and newsletters get your messages out to a highly targeted group of readers. Both are effective because they are timely, published regularly, and easy to read. However, newsletters can eat up a lot of cash, particularly for printing and distribution. But if a newsletter makes sense for your business, make sure yours has lots of pictures, white space, pull-out quotes, and sidebars to enhance readability and keep your readers interested.

New links must be forged as old ones rust.
JANE HOWARD

To reach new and wider audiences with your promotional efforts, consider partnering with other businesses. You can partner with suppliers, other like-minded businesses or nonprofits, or believe it or not, your competition.

For example, all the shoe stores in town could jointly sponsor the 10-K race that raises money for the homeless shelter or for the American Cancer Society. You could put together a coalition of businesses to sponsor events like First Night on New Year's Eve. Or you could do what Ben and Jerry's ice cream and Stoneyfield Yogurt do and donate a percentage of your profits to protecting the environment

Shopinprivate.com is a Michigan-based Web site doing a brisk business selling items most of us feel uncomfortable buying: Preparation H, douches, pregnancy tests, breath drops, adult toys and more. President Thomas Nardone faced the challenge of how to market the site, since it isn't the kind customers will generally tell others they bought from. He decided that the best bet was to target college students. Coeds need condoms, tampons, lubricants and other assorted sundries, but are still young enough to squirm when they go to a store to buy the stuff. Nardone purchased a mailing list of 800 college newspapers and faxed a press release to each of them. Now half the site's traffic is from college students. (*Success*, April 1999, page 23)

> Trade groups and community-based business groups can be gold mines of information—if you know how to extract the riches from them. Groups on a smaller and less formal scale can also provide big payoffs. One is the Digital Dames, a group of female executives in Silicon Valley. The Dames meet every six weeks or so, moving from house to house but never varying the format of their meetings. They all sit down and introduce themselves, saying what they need at the moment—whether it's advice, people on their board, employees, or money. Support is given, ideas are shared, e-mail addresses are exchanged, plans are made, deals are cut.

or other worthy cause. This is what's called cause-related marketing, and it gives your customers yet another reason to buy your product or service over that of your competition.

Mr. Morgan buys his partners; I grow my own.

ANDREW CARNEGIE

Partnering with organizations is not only a great way to make new business contacts—it can also lead to great satisfaction on the personal level as well. Sponsoring a little league baseball team or having your staff spend a few hours every week as a big brother or sister isn't just good PR for your company—it brings great benefits for both the kids and the adults who participate.

Volunteer somewhere. Opportunities abound at schools, hospitals, public broadcasting stations, libraries, and lots of community service organizations. You could also become a trustee of a nonprofit group whose mission you're committed to. Not only do you get your name out where people begin to recognize it—you also do a tremendous service for the organization you're working for, which in most circumstances, has a tight budget and limited financial resources.

If you have lots of experience in your field, consider becoming a mentor or advisor to someone who's just starting out. You can put the word out through your local chamber of commerce, through your local business school, or via your own grapevine. You could also contact your local Small Business Administration's

SCORE (Service Corps of Retired Executives) program—they may be able to match you with new entrepreneurs who could benefit from your advice.

If you can't find a group that meets your needs, consider starting a peer-to-peer mentoring group of your own. You could meet every month and pair up in "teams" of two for that month. This way, everyone in the group will have an opportunity to work with everyone else and reap the benefits of the group's diverse skills, resources, and points of view.

> *By their fruits ye shall know them.*
>
> MATTHEW 7:20

Another way to expand your group of contacts is to network. You can do this informally (over lunch, coffee, or the telephone) or more formally at events and trade shows. But before you do this kind of networking, make sure you've thought through what to say about yourself and your work, so you're prepared to chat with anyone you meet. Remember to use your best manners, dress professionally, and limit your alcohol intake. Schmooze, but save your sales pitches for later.

If you're the shy type, take along a friend who has the gift of gab. Working with you as a team, his or her mission would be to break the ice and help you meet new people.

The goal of networking isn't to see how many people you can meet in an hour. The idea is to gather information and work on compiling a list of people you can count on. Before you attend a big event, set

While running an Office of Economic Opportunity agency in Burlington, Vermont, Hal Colston saw the importance of cars to his clients—jobless people couldn't find work because they could not afford a car, and public transportation was often skimpy. He first shared his idea of a "community garage" with Frederick Neu, his Lutheran pastor, and then with the congregation. Both were so enthusiastic that the Good News Garage was quickly born in 1996, thanks to support from Lutheran Social Services. Cars are donated to the Garage, which it then sells to customers for the cost of repairs. Seventy-five percent of clients referred to the Garage have subsequently gotten off welfare and 60 communities across the country want community garages of their own. (*Smithsonian*, January 1999, pages 90-100)

Bill Leeson, a former documentary filmmaker in London, has created a new breed of nonprofit—one that combines good works with smart business. War Child is the organization he co-founded six years ago to aid children in strife-torn regions. It has delivered nearly $13 million of aid and services to young people in the former Yugoslavia and in Africa—with a staff of just 15 that operates on a lean four-percent overhead. Part of War Child's media success has been the result of connections: It helps to have friends in the media who control the cameras. Leeson works with them to generate compelling footage and dramatic stories. He has three criteria for evaluating projects for War Child. "First, is it needed? Second, does it duplicate other efforts? Third, can I publicize it? You can't raise money without awareness." (*Fast Company*, "Do-Gooders Need Not Apply," June 1999, pages 50-52)

goals—for example, to meet several prospective customers or someone who has a business just like yours—and try to achieve them.

Here in New Hampshire, our local chambers of commerce sponsor Business After Hours nights several times a year. These events are great ways to meet other business owners or prospective customers in your community and find out what's on their minds.

You can also network one-on-one by asking a colleague or friend to introduce you to someone you'd like to get to know. Since people respond best to initial contacts from people they already know, don't overlook this valuable networking resource.

It's not whom you know but how you are known to them.

THEODORE LEVITT

---

10 How Do You Advertise Your Products and Services?

When should you advertise? There are three times: when business is good, when business is not good, and all times in between. The two main advertising problems afflicting small business owners are caused by trying to do it themselves (advertising is a highly skilled profession) and not running advertising campaigns (trying to make a single ad take the place of a series of ads).

Clarity, consistency, and customer knowledge are all necessary for proper communication. Don't try to do it yourself. You have other tasks that you are better off performing.

I do not read advertisements—
I would spend all my time wanting things.
ARCHBISHOP OF CANTERBURY

Wendy Kury, director of marketing for Graphito, an advertising and marketing communications agency in Portsmouth, New Hampshire, hands out a sheet with some ideas and questions to her new and prospective clients. Her intention is to inform them what is involved *before* making promotional decisions.

1. *Media.* What have you used and/or are presently using for promotional materials? Are you happy with them? What kind of response have you received?
2. *Target audience.* Whom are you trying to reach? Focus the target segment as much as possible, as if you are talking to one person.
3. *Advertising objective.* What are you trying to accomplish? What problems are you trying to solve? It may be an image problem, a location problem, or an awareness problem. It is always a problem advertising can help correct. What will be the result? Be single-minded; do not be too general.
4. *Primary benefit.* What is the single most important point about your product/service? If you say only one thing about your product, what would it be? Is there something that makes your product better or different than the rest?
5. *Supporting reasons why.* Anyone can say they are the best…back it up!
6. *Competitive environment.* Who are your competitors? What are their claims? What are their weaknesses?
7. *Executing considerations.* Do you need/like/want four-color, two-color, black-and-white, a coupon, an 800-number, a response device?
8. *Time frame.* When do you need it? No, when do you *really* need it?
9. *Budget.* What are your cost considerations?

Before beginning to run advertising, figure out where your target markets are on the promotional pyramid.

1. Acts
2. Convinced
3. Comprehends
4. Aware of your company
5. Unaware of your company

Ads alone can't present the right message to the right market at the right time without forethought. The promotional pyramid breaks this process down into customer-centered steps. The key: You can move your markets along only one step at a time.

Step One: Most of the consuming public have no idea that you are in business. When you defined your target markets, you made moving these markets up one step much easier. This first step is easily overlooked. You and your pals know that you are in business, but does the target market? If not, the first thing to do is make them aware that you are indeed in business.

This is where "grand openings" and media blitzes are most helpful. They create awareness in wide markets. Although you want your message (Here we are! Hello!) to focus on your target markets, awareness ads can profitably reach a wider audience.

Step Two: Now your markets are aware that you are in business. Do they know what you do? Are they aware of the full range of products and services you provide? Most likely not. Unless you are positive that your markets really know what you do, your ad

In the 1980s steel makers had invested $50 billion to make steel lighter, cheaper and of higher quality. But if consumers didn't understand steel's benefits, they might not demand the material in the products they bought. The Steel Alliance and its ad agency developed several television commercials. One showed a diver in an underwater steel cage surrounded by menacing sharks. Others were concerned with safety and environmental themes. Within the campaign's first year, public awareness of steel and its products jumped from 13 to 26 percent. Positive mentions of the steel industry had risen to 78 percent, up from 24 percent the previous year. Negative mentions fell to one percent from 37 percent. (*American Demographics*, March 1999, page 56)

should convey the message, "This is what we do, what we sell, carry, provide." Remember: One step at a time.

Step Three: This is the *positioning* step, the one in which you try to stand out from the competition as providing your markets with the best solutions to their needs and problems. Your implicit message in this step is: "We're the best, have the right knowledge, skills, quality, value for you—and here's how come." Here is where you sell benefits that are valued by the target market.

Most persons new to business focus on this step and ignore the awareness and comprehension steps, then wonder why their ad doesn't work.

Step Four: The last step is to persuade the convinced to take action, now, to buy the product, visit your store or Web site, try a sample, or take whatever action you want them to take. Here is where persuasion comes into play. Those ads you see or hear that cry "One day only! Last chance! Buy now!" are action ads. The action should be specific and simple, easy for them to take. Toll-free numbers, response cards, and coupons can help.

The key: You can move your markets along but one step at a time. Know your markets—and then choose the right message.

Advertising is the place where the
selfish interests of the manufacturer coincide
with the interests of society.

DAVID OGILVY

AIDA is not an opera, though some of us feel it is a work of art. It's an old acronym, similar in message to the promotion pyramid.

"A" stands for getting their Attention. "I" for piquing their Interest. "D" for arousing their Desire, or for helping them Decide. "A" for moving them to Act.

One step at a time. And keep it simple.

Advertising is easy to do poorly, difficult to do well—and low-cost, do-it-yourself ads often turn out to be the most expensive of all in the long run. Think of advertising as an investment in future profits.

Use a professional. A small agency will be a better fit for a small business, and you may even be able to barter for services. In any case, there are ways to lower the initial cost.

Ascertain your target market's media preferences. What papers, magazines, and journals do they read? What television and radio shows appeal to them? Are they a computer-literate lot?

Make sure the message is consistent with your desired image.

Gear the tone and message to your audience. This presupposes that you can tell the agency who the market is and how the message might best be presented. A television ad for a law firm targeting unsophisticated accident victims has quite a different feel from a newspaper ad for corporate legal clients. Fit the message to the market.

If you know the "hot buttons," the emotional triggers of your markets, press them. Poignancy pays.

An ad agency has to know these things before they can prepare ad campaigns that will achieve your

Using coded messages, more mainstream companies are targeting gay consumers. On billboards and buses, Subaru models have bumper stickers showing a blue-and-yellow equal sign, the logo of the Human Rights Campaign, a gay advocacy group. In ads with the slogan—"Different Drivers. Different Roads. One Car"—the Subaru cars also have vanity plates, XENA LVR and P-TOWNIE. (Translation: The TV show *Xena: Warrior Princess* has a large lesbian following; P-TOWNIE refers to Provincetown, a gay mecca on Cape Cod.) (*The Wall Street Journal*, June 29, 1999)

goals. They can discover them at $150 an hour—or you can discover them yourself.

Butterflies come to pretty flowers.
KOREAN PROVERB

What medium would be best for your market? There are innumerable ways to advertise, ranging from inexpensive local papers and small yellow pages ads, to national television and national magazines. Your budget is one constraint but not necessarily the most important.

Print media includes newspapers, magazines, newsletters, brochures, inserts, blow-ins, direct mail, and anything printed that can be used to advertise your business. Even balloons and matchbooks, packaging and pens.

Electronic media includes public and commercial radio and television.

E-commerce (the Internet) is growing explosively. The impact of the computer on all media, not just e-commerce, is stunning. (See Chapter 14 for more information.)

Other media includes billboards, sandwich boards, sky writing, give-away specialties of all kinds. The list is endless.

No matter what medium you choose, make sure it is one that your markets appreciate.

Doing business without advertising is like winking at a girl in the dark. You know what you're doing but no one else does.

STEWARD H. BRITT

The Internet is a formidable advertising medium for small businesses. Some claim that it has "leveled the playing field" (don't believe it!) between large and small businesses. We won't go that far, but a thoughtful use of e-commerce is certainly in your interest. The trick is not to squander time and money trying to appear au courant.

Visit these Web sites to see how some small businesses use e-commerce, plus some huge ones:

- *www.yaz.com* is a small specialty retailer.
- *www.retailernews.com* is for retailers wishing inspirational stories and sales advice.
- *www.amazon.com* bills itself as "the world's biggest bookstore."
- *www.golfballs.com* wholesales golf balls.
- *www.smalloffice.com* is the Web site for *Small Business Computing* and *Home Office Computing* magazines.
- *www.dell.com* belongs to Dell Computers, the first company to sell computers directly to consumers, and has information on products, technology consulting services, and more.

Willy Hills, owner of Limitless Design of Somerville, Massachusetts, ascertained that his clients were primarily college and graduate school graduates interested in the artistic and cultural life the Boston area provides so abundantly. He decided to advertise his semi-custom wood furniture in *Symphony Notes* (the Boston Symphony Orchestra's playbill) and in alumni magazines. His decision was excellent. For a small fraction of the cost of advertising in the Boston newspapers, his previous medium, he reached his target audience in an uncluttered and favorable environment.

- *www.popswine.com* sells specialty wines and spirits.
- *www.marketnet.com* specializes in Web site development.
- *www.marketing-source.com* offers marketing support for Internet and brick-and-mortar businesses.
- *www.smallbusiness.yahoo.com* provides tips on building e-mail lists.
- *www.smallbizhelp.net* is the Small Business Resource and Help Center.
- *www.morebusiness.com* is the Business Resource Center.
- *www.nbia.org* is the National Business Incubation Association.
- *www.sba.gov* is the U.S. Small Business Administration.

However far modern science and technics have fallen short of their inherent possibilities, they have taught mankind at least one lesson: nothing is impossible.

Lewis Mumford

Don't fall for the temptingly low-priced exercise of designing your business card on your computer. A well-designed business card is an effective advertisement for your business if it is designed with your market in mind. Be professional.

What might go on your card?

Information should include your name, title, address, phone and fax numbers, e-mail, and Web site. Backup phone numbers are always important.

Regarding typography, different typefaces present different images. Times New Roman says traditional. Zapf Dingbat does not!

Then there are graphics. Andy's card has a representation of Thud, his ancient and beloved black Lab. His former card, when he worked with banks, looked like a banker's card. Not whimsical, not fun. But very acceptable to people who wear dark suits.

Our friend Bert Myer, a marketing consultant to several large companies and also to the U.S. Croquet Association, has a card that simply says "Bert" in large green letters. His numbers and addresses are in black, lowercase.

If you aren't knowledgeable about how to put these graphic and typographic elements to work for you, be careful. It's easy to send the wrong image.

Some cards use humor. Some do not. It depends on your markets and your personality. What result do you want to achieve? A laugh or a place in their Rolodex?

Speaking of Rolodex, some people use die-cut cards that can go immediately into a Rolodex.

Now that many business owners use scanners, it may be more important than ever that your card be legible to an OCR reader. That way your prospects can scan your card directly into their computer, ready at a keystroke for future reference.

Foldover and outsize cards are sometimes useful, especially by salespeople who use them as mini-brochures. The drawback is that they don't fit into a Rolodex or a standard format, and may be discarded as another piece of litter.

Our pal Bert Myer, a marketing consultant who includes Polaroid and other large companies among his clients, makes sure that his clients and prospects remember him by sending out ballpoint pens (sometimes expensive, sometimes not), baseball caps, and other wee gifts every now and then. These are all emblazoned BERT, a simple effective reminder that if you want your business to be remembered, call BERT. His postcards, also promoting BERT, are classics—Bert poses with statues, for example, or on his croquet lawn where he carefully tromps out BERT in large letters in the dew. Think marketing? Think BERT!

What do you want your business card to do? Be a silent salesperson for you? Then treat it as an important piece of your advertising mix.

I believe that it is better to be looked over than it is to be overlooked.

MAE WEST

Advertising does not have to cost a lot of money. Some of the most effective small business ads are very inexpensive.

Word-of-mouth advertising is often misunderstood. It cannot be passive if it is to be effective. You have to ask customers and friends and acquaintances for referrals—ask them to tell their pals about what a good job you do. Andy's current favorite radio station's sole advertising asks listeners to "tell a friend about AM 1380." He heard of it from his mother-in-law. Happy customers are glad to tell others—but need to be reminded.

Send thank-you notes. Everyone likes to be appreciated. This will make you stand out from the crowd.

Send birthday and holiday cards. A specialty fruit merchant in Vermont includes a card asking for birthdates (but not the year) in each order. This has become their best way to keep in touch with their invaluable repeat customers.

The bulletin board approach to advertising can be effective for some businesses, especially very local services. The local grocery store provides a free spot to place an ad, pin up a business card. Some even encourage small businesses to leave their brochures on a table so the market's customers get another (if ancillary) service.

Be ingenious. Keep your eyes open for how other small businesses advertise. Once you start looking, you'll be surprised at the range of clever ideas people use to promote their businesses.

A little goes a long way.

AMERICAN PROVERB

Don't limit your telephone ads to the yellow pages. Get listed in special directories, business-to-business phone books, and other sources of telephone numbers. Use your Web site to spread the word of your phone number. Include it in your ads, mailings, brochures, flyers, and other materials. Even on your packaging. Your customers will appreciate not having to look up the number whenever they might wish to call you.

800- and 888-numbers serve a special purpose. They make it easy and convenient for customers to get in touch with you. There are some services that will take this a step further and provide a way for customers to order by phone any time of the day, any day of the year. You don't have to be on the phone 24/7 to provide this easy convenience to your customers.

A word of advice: The phone is so important that you should train all of your employees who might answer calls in basic telephone etiquette, and make sure that appropriate information is next to every phone.

The Internet is an advertiser's dream in many ways. The best ads are informative (see page 174) and the

Handwritten postcards grab attention. At Upstart Publishing Company, we called these "Andygrams." We used them to introduce new services and products, offer congratulations, thank people for being customers and referral sources, and for any other reason we could think up. The personal touch is a great ad in itself. Inexpensive premiums, carefully chosen and given to carefully chosen prospects, can also work wonders. Upstart gained a major customer (Cornell University) when a professor at the Hotel School spotted one of Andy's children with an Upstart polo shirt. Professor Peter Rainsford inquired, Andy shipped—and since then Peter has written two best-selling books with Andy, as well as introduced his material to the broader Cornell community. Not bad for a $20 premium.

A greater percentage of General Motors' Buick division's advertising money now goes toward Web projects. When Buick offered an e-coupon for $500 off the purchase price of a Buick Regal, more than 25 percent of Regal's retail sales in a three-month period were sold with the e-coupon. That was a much better rate of leads resulting in sales than the minuscule returns from typical direct-mail appeals. (*The Wall Street Journal*, July 6, 1999)

Internet allows you to present a huge amount of information for little cost.

Think of it this way. People who visit your Web site do so either because they sought it out (used a search engine, or even entered your URL) or because they stumbled upon it. If your site is of interest to them, they'll stay on to read your messages, save the site for a later visit, send it to friends who might be interested in what you have for sale.

The audience, in other words, qualifies itself. If they stay at your site, they may be ready to buy, so provide that option. These are great prospects, so you will want to capture their names and address. Therefore:

- Ask visitors to ask questions and post comments.
- Offer something—a contest, a "special report," an electronic newspaper, an electronic clipping, notice of special sales or events, discounts on selected products.
- Promise to send them information of similar sites. Position yourself as their ally, not as a mere supplier.

Visit *www.ecrc.uofs.edu* for more e-commerce advertising ideas.

Your goal is to tailor the contents of your Web site to the point in the buying cycle where you can most efficiently communicate with your market.

ROGER C. PARKER

Direct mail is a special kind of advertising used successfully by many small businesses. It's a very difficult art to practice since it has many variables, but properly executed it is self-correcting.

Why is it hard? You have to do almost all the selling in the direct-mail package. You have to select a mailing list composed of real prospects for your products. You have to offer these people a variety of products to choose from. Single-item mailings are too risky. Since returns of one to two percent are considered the norm, there is not much room for error. Though Andi may buy a dibbler to plant tulips with tomorrow, she isn't interested today. But she may be in the mood for a secateur.

There are great advantages. This is a very well studied form of retail. Visit your library—books by experts like Robert Bly, Maxwell Sroge, and others are excellent how-to's.

We paid a visit to Amazon.com and searched for "direct mail" and found more than 150 books. Top matches for this search:

1. *The Complete Direct Marketing Sourcebook: A Step-By-Step Guide to Organizing and Managing a Successful Direct Marketing Program* by John Kremer
2. *Designing Direct Mail That Sells* by Sandra J. Blum
3. *Building a Mail Order Business: A Complete Manual for Success, 4th Edition,* by William A. Cohen

When Dell Computer Corporation started selling computers by catalogues, it was scoffed at by analysts, because consumers were not expected to make such expensive purchases by catalogue. However, by offering low prices and proven technology, Dell has managed to become one of the most profitable personal computer sellers in the low-margin, cut-throat computer market. It now offers sub-$1,000 PCs, along with printers and leasing plans to keep the lower-priced machines from lowering profit. Tapping this market continues the company's practice of sidestepping first-time computer buyers. (*The Wall Street Journal*, April 6, 1999)

These experts will show you how to put together a package (letter, offer, response device) suited to your market, choose mailing lists, even find sources of product. You will learn how to test one package against another, each time going forward with the better package or better list, discarding those that don't draw. You will learn how to test a statistically significant fraction of a large list, an affordable way to test out your ideas about your markets.

Make no mistake. This is hard work, advertising and retail of a very high order. If you approach it in small steps, patiently and with discipline, it will work for you.

The advertisement is one of the most interesting and difficult of modern literary forms.

ALDOUS HUXLEY

One novel way to see if your product will find a market is to offer it on one of the big Internet auction sites. This will show you what one segment of the populace thinks your product is worth—in real dollars, not just in subjective, "Well, I like it" terms.

The signs you put up, window displays, point-of-purchase displays are all forms of advertising. They should reflect the message and image that you wish to portray.

- Do they reinforce your other ads?
- Do they use the typeface and logotype that your other ads use?

- Do they invite people in?
- Do they clearly show what your business is?

You have plenty of chances to use signs, inside and out. Make sure they work for you, not against you.

Many a small thing has been made large by the right kind of advertising.

MARK TWAIN

Packaging is often a critical concern at the point of purchase. L'Eggs hosiery is a classic, eye-catching, point-of-purchase display, with its hundreds of plastic eggs in different colors. DIM, a French hosiery manufacturer and subsidiary of the BIC Company, took the fashion hosiery market by storm with its patterned, silky textured stockings that were displayed in a patented package with a hole through which a swatch of the stocking protruded. The package allowed the shopper not just to see but feel "la difference." (Peter R. Dickson, *Marketing Management*, Fort Worth: The Dryden Press, 1994, page 320)

11

How Do You Sell Your Products and Services?

Selling and marketing are not the same. Although marketing is mostly involved with educating current and prospective customers about your product or service, sales involves actually getting that product or service into customers' hands. Because of its direct impact on your company's bottom line, your method of sales and distribution is one of the most important aspects of your business.

But sales don't just happen and no matter how great your product or service is, it cannot sell itself. To sell successfully, your business needs a sales strategy, trained personnel to implement it, and sales management.

Your sales strategy involves finding prospects and letting them know about your product or service. It also involves determining which product or service features you'll emphasize in order to get customers to buy; whether your sales efforts are local, national, or international; and whether you'll employ traditional or innovative techniques in order to sell your product or service.

Sales training for your staff is an investment that ultimately produces a more profitable return for your company. Whereas basic sales training increases a salesperson's general competence, company-specific training makes that employee more valuable in his or her current position at your company. It also increases that person's loyalty to your company and decreases turnover.

The key to Gallo Wines' merchandising success is its concern with details. Its distributors are required to employ separate Gallo representatives who build floor displays, lift cases, and dust bottles. These reps operate according to a 300-page training and sales manual. Topics in it include sales calls and maintaining shelves. Other advice the reps are given: to place the most highly advertised Gallo products at eye level, to place impulse purchase items on shelves above the belt, and to make the display area no wider than seven feet (the largest width the eye can scan). (Peter R. Dickson, *Marketing Management*, Fort Worth: The Dryden Press, 1994, page 345)

Sales management, which is one of your top priorities as business owner, involves planning for key markets, determining sales strategies, and motivating your sales force. If you're not a natural-born inspirational leader, there are plenty of courses to take or audio and videotapes to buy that can help you improve your motivational skills. Motivational speaker Zig Ziglar is a prolific producer of books and tapes—Amazon.com lists more than 60!

There is no such thing as "soft sell" and "hard sell." There is only "smart sell" and "stupid sell."

CHARLES BROWER

Direct marketing refers to anything that attempts to make a sale right then and there—mail order, direct mail, coupon advertising, telemarketing, direct-response TV, postcard decks, door-to-door salespeople, home shopping, and Internet shopping.

Many companies use direct mail to find prospective customers. Thanks to computers, mailing lists can be customized according to any number of classifications: by demographic data, by frequency of purchase, by amount of purchase, and so on. Lists can be cleaned up via the software's merge-and-purge feature, which helps prevent duplication and sending mailings to people who don't want to receive them. Letters can be personalized, in the salutation as well as in the body copy.

The biggest users of direct mail are magazine publishers, catalog houses, food stores, department stores, and book clubs. The two biggest advantages of direct mail are that results of the mailing can be measured and that different variables of the mailing can be tested. These include the way the product is positioned, its price, terms of payment, what (if anything) is offered to entice the reader to respond, the expiration date for an offer, and the format of the mailing.

In *Ogilvy on Advertising*, advertising guru David Ogilvy talks about a highbrow magazine that tested terms of payment for subscriptions. In one, the subscriber was asked to pay $65 for 56 issues. In another, $42.50 for 39 issues. In the third, $29.95 for 29 issues. Although it cut the price 40 percent, the third generated 35 percent more net revenue.

Other tips Ogilvy offers: Long copy sells more than short copy, testimonials increase credibility and sales, and short words work best.

In baiting a mouse trap with cheese,
always leave room for the mouse.

SAKI

But direct mail isn't only for large companies. Small businesses can use direct mail to their advantage as well—either to generate leads or to make sales.

The key with any direct-mail campaign is the mailing list. It must be accurate, up-to-date, and suit your purposes. If you don't have your own list, you can buy one from a list broker (look under "mailing lists" in the yellow pages). Just make sure the list is the right one for your purposes.

According to the U.S. Postal Service, companies send out more than 77 billion pieces of direct mail each year. One example is the Harley Davidson Motor Company. All new owners are provided with an automatic one-year membership in the Harley Owners' Group (HOG). Throughout the year, magazines, newsletters, and other communications that build camaraderie among riders are sent to them. HOG boasts more than 400,000 members. An impressive 75 percent of them respond to direct-mail solicitations and pay a $40 fee to continue their memberships.

Your direct-mail campaign may be as simple as letters mailed weekly or monthly. Postcards are even more effective because their offers are concise, their mail costs are lower, and they're easy to produce and print on computers. Postcards are great for saying thanks to valued customers, reminding clients of their next appointment, and announcing a sale, discount, or new service. To really grab a reader's attention, consider using oversized or color postcards.

Used by Ben Franklin to sell books in 1744, catalogs are more complicated direct-mail vehicles. Consumers love them because they're convenient and make shopping from home easy, thanks to 24-hour service seven days a week and 800-numbers.

Not only do catalogs need to offer the right merchandise to the right market, they also need to have the right graphics, the right use of color, be the right size, and have the right copy, the right sales stimulators, and the right order forms. They should always include an order form, along with an offer for a gift for purchases of, say, $50 or more. The company's 800-number should be on every page of the catalog.

Keep in mind that with any type of direct mail, single mailings aren't nearly as effective as mailings with follow-ups, and that mailings with phone follow-ups are best of all.

Countless books and articles have been written about the subject of direct mail. One is *Successful Direct Marketing Methods* by Bob Stone, published by Crain Books in Chicago. Jay Conrad Levenson's *Guerrilla Marketing* has a helpful chapter. On the Web, check out Direct Mail World at *www.dmworld.com* and

Direct Mail News at *www.dmnews.com*. But if your campaign is looking like a complicated one, you're best served by getting in touch with a direct-mail professional.

He that speaks ill of the mare will buy her.
BEN FRANKLIN

Direct-response marketing involves advertisements on television and in magazines that invite people to send their orders directly to you, without going to a store.

As in print advertising, the headline is the most important element. Make sure it offers a benefit to the reader. Good photographs help sell products, as do testimonials and well-organized layouts. Coupons should be miniature versions of your ad since readers usually skip to coupons to see what the offer is. To compel readers to act now instead of later, entice them with the words "limited offer," "limited supply," or "last time at this price."

If you code your coupon, you'll know how many orders came from each insertion in each publication. One magazine might perform twice as well as another, which can make a difference in your bottom line.

Pay attention to where your competition runs ads and continues to run them. Also watch for editorial changes in the publication you're advertising in—they can attract or repel readers.

I was successful because you believed in me.
ULYSSES S. GRANT

Teenage girls spend $70 billion every year, and MXG Media Inc. wants a part of that. The company sells clothes and accessories via the Internet and a hybrid publication known as a "magalog," part magazine, part catalog, which is sent to 500,000 girls every quarter. The two-year-old company projects that it will triple its $4 million revenues in 1999, a success that results from staying close to the customer. It hires teen girls, paying them $7 an hour, to work after school answering letters, doing interviews, and punching up copy to make it sound, like, y'know, authentic. No word goes to print without a teen girl first checking it. "Being uncool is the kiss of death in this business," says CEO Hunter Heaney. (*Forbes*, May 31, 1999, page 130)

Telephone marketing generates a surprising number of sales—more than half of all goods and services sold in 1997 were sold by phone. It also costs about one-third as much as direct mail.

Telephone marketing is often used in conjunction with direct-mail programs as a follow-up. It can be done by you and members of your staff, or be hired out to a firm that specializes in it.

Telemarketing accounts for almost half of all direct-mail purchases for businesses selling to other businesses. The successful telemarketers plan the entire phone call and the follow-up. Since they know that they have only a few seconds before losing a person's attention, they give a good reason for their call right away: to help you motivate staff, boost profits, improve image, manage cash flow, attain a competitive edge, and so on.

Before calling a number, successful telemarketers find out what they need to know about the prospect, how to get him or her to take action, how to deal with the person screening calls (a secretary or assistant), what to say in a voice-mail message. We advise that you memorize, rather than read from, a script, changing any words that don't quite feel natural to you. Practice by using a tape recorder. Speak naturally, with assurance, and direct the conversation to the customer's needs. Ask lots of questions, so the person won't feel talked at. And know how you'll handle objections, which often turn out to be opportunities in disguise.

One of the best ways to persuade others is with your ears—by listening to them.

DEAN RUSK

Telephone marketing isn't just your calling customers or prospects—it can also be customers calling you via a toll-free or a 900-number, both of which are usually the provenance of larger companies.

A toll-free number can dramatically increase a response rate—by 30 percent or more. Many companies request 800-numbers whose digits correspond to their seven-letter company name or product. Although this gives customers an easy way to remember the number, it takes more time and effort to dial. Consequently, there's nothing wrong with a toll-free number of seven arbitrary numbers. If customers have forgotten or misplaced your number, they can call toll-free information at 800-555-1212.

Although 900-numbers have been associated with porn and scams, many "kosher" companies like Procter & Gamble have successfully used them. Callers do not mind paying the dialing fee because they get something in return, such as a product sample or a coupon for a discount on a purchase. The advantages of having a 900-number are that your prospects are hot (they spent money to find out about your company!) and if you use a service called Prizm 900, available from your local phone company, you can categorize callers by 40 different demographic and psychographic clusters.

Where you sell your wares has been profoundly—and permanently—affected by the Internet. The amount of Web commerce took off in 1998, achieving in the single month of August what everyone thought it would take the entire year to do. According to The Wall Street Journal (May 18,

Ellett Brothers Inc. in Chapin, South Carolina, is one of the nation's biggest wholesale gun distributors. It dominates the $2 billion gun industry, along with about a dozen rivals that have adopted its incentive-based telemarketing approach. Sales of gun and ammunition at Ellett totaled nearly $75 million in 1998. New hires go through eight weeks of gun training and two weeks of instruction on sales and self-motivation techniques. With gun sales of all types down sharply since 1994, Ellett has emphasized ways to deal with rejection and has taught its salespeople to always suggest add-ons, like holsters, before hanging up. (*The Wall Street Journal*, April 21, 1999, A-1)

Getting a new e-commerce Web site off the ground costs, on average, $1 million, according to Gartner-Group in Stamford, Connecticut. It studied 20 companies and found they had budgeted only 50 percent to 75 percent of what actual costs were. Labor was the biggest expense, making up 79 percent of the costs. Brookstone Inc., a specialty retailer based in Nashua, New Hampshire, wasn't surprised. It went through three technology partners from 1996 to 1999. The biggest shock: translating catalogue images into digital data. All the product photos had to be reworked. The company also spent a year negotiating to buy rights to the domain name Brookstone.com, which was already taken. (*The Wall Street Journal*, May 27, 1999, A-1)

1999, A-4), online retail sales are expected to double in 1999 to $11.04 billion. The percentage of total sales from the Internet, including sales to consumers and businesses, is expected to increase about 50 percent annually through 2004. Total retail sales are expected to grow about a paltry 3.6 percent a year in comparison.

E-commerce has made shopping a heck of a lot more convenient. According to America Online, most online shopping takes place between 10 pm and 10 am, long after most stores are closed.

E-commerce has become such a force to be reckoned with that Carnegie Mellon University in Pittsburgh now offers a masters degree program in electronic commerce. The program is a response to requests from companies like Sun Microsystems and IBM, who need to think about how they compete on the Internet—not just how to compete in general. Other business schools following suit include MIT's Sloan School of Management, Vanderbilt, the University of Maryland, and Creighton University.

But e-commerce isn't just about how to use the Internet and fancy technology. It's about getting products from the warehouse to the consumer and still making money. How do you accomplish that, when companies like Amazon.com have continued to operate at a loss while selling millions of dollars of merchandise?

A salesman has got to dream, boy.
It comes with the territory.
ARTHUR MILLER, DEATH OF A SALESMAN

In his critically acclaimed book Roger C. Parker's Guide to Web Content and Design (IDG Books Worldwide, 1997), the best-selling author and pal of ours says that eight elements are involved in making a Web site successful. Parker emphasizes that all eight deserve equal attention.

- First is planning: Know what you want the site to do for you.
- Second is content: Make sure it's well organized and well presented, so people will return to your site on a regular basis.
- Third is design: The graphics should be pleasant to look at and used to effectively deliver the site's message to a targeted audience.
- Fourth is involvement: Know what you want people to do when they visit your site and afterward.
- Fifth is production: How will your site be created and posted on the Internet?
- Sixth is follow-up: Don't make people wait after they've contacted you, or ignore them altogether.
- Seventh is promotion: Let people know, both online and offline, about your site.
- Eighth is maintenance: A Web site should be in a state of constant improvement.

To travel hopefully is a better thing than to arrive,
and the true success is to labour.

ROBERT LOUIS STEVENSON

Analysts expect Amazon.com's sales to top $1.4 billion in 1999, and it has added music, video, gifts, and greeting cards to the books it offers some 8.4 million customers—along with links to drugstore goods, pet supplies and more. But in a move to compete with its biggest online rival, Barnesandnoble.com, it now offers 50 percent discounts on some 70 best-selling books every week. To some extent, Amazon is treating these best sellers as loss leaders that attract customers into its online store, where they can be tempted by other merchandise that isn't priced so cheaply. (*Business Week*, "eBay vs. Amazon.com," May 31, 1999, and *The Wall Street Journal*, May 17, 1999, B-11)

Customers who work with CarsDirect.com will never have to talk to a car dealer, if they so choose. Instead, CarsDirect gives consumers a set price online based on recent average selling prices. It works through existing dealers to get the car at those prices, and delivers vehicles to buyers' homes or offices. (*The Wall Street Journal*, May 17, 1999, B-4)

If you're interested in setting up a Web site for your business and you're technologically inclined, pick up a copy of Roger's book. But if you're technologically challenged, help is only a phone call or click away. The Massachusetts Software Council lists nearly 40 companies involved in online services, such as Net consulting, and another 90 involved in some aspect of Web site design, development, and support. Your local chamber of commerce might be able to recommend Web designers in your area. So might ad agencies, computer user groups, and other business organizations.

Other ways of getting products into customers' hands include multilevel marketing, also known as network sales or MLM, franchises, or directly to the customer (referred to as the "Dell model" because Dell Computers sells directly to consumers via the Internet). MLMs can be tricky because not only do salespeople sell the product but they also recruit others who in turn sell the product and recruit other salespeople. By all means, avoid any that appear to be unscrupulous pyramid schemes.

With both MLMs and franchises, it's imperative that you do your homework. Check the organization's financial statements, years in business, management team, and industry standing. Analyze the position of the product in its industry, and see how the marketing and training provided by the company stacks up to others. Check also with your state's attorney general's office and your Better Business Bureau to get more information.

For more information on franchises, contact:

- The American Franchisee Association in Chicago at 312-431-1467, *infonews.com/franchise/wif*
- The U.S. Federal Trade Commission at *www.ftc.gov* for *The Consumer's Guide to Buying a Franchise*
- The International Franchise Association in Washington, D.C., at 202-628-8000, *www.franchise.org*

I come from a state that raises corn and cotton and cockleburs and Democrats, and frothy eloquence neither convinces nor satisfies me. I am from Missouri. You have got to show me.

WILLARD DUNCAN VANDIVER, 1899

Regardless of how you get your product or service into your customer's hands, you need to plan your after-sale follow-up. If you don't provide adequate service after making your sale, your customers could end up buying from your competition.

What kind of follow-up should you do? Direct mail (a letter or a post card) is a low-cost option, and it works. So do phone calls. If you have a service desk, make sure it's staffed with employees who are polite and knowledgeable. Establish a return policy that favors the customer.

Follow-up differentiates your business from your competitors'. Satisfied customers talk. But not as much as unsatisfied customers—and they complain to an average of 11 other people. That's powerful negative word-of-mouth publicity!

> Steve Siegel is a Dunkin' Donuts franchisee with 35 units in Boston. Before he buys property, he and his assistants count pedestrians. They want people headed for the office who need coffee now, not the leisurely shoppers more inclined to go to Starbucks. One of his top spots is a mere 64 square feet, for which he pays $30,000 a year in rent. "When you get into saturated areas, you have to get creative," says Mr. Siegel, who is scheduled to become chair of the International Franchise Association in 2002. (*The Wall Street Journal*, May 11, 1999, B-2)

Dell Computer has grown rapidly because it maintains a direct relationship with the end users of its products, which are custom-configured and sold at reasonable prices, and its service and support. Since customer satisfaction is dogma at Dell Computer, industry-leading warranty packages, installation, maintenance, repair services and user support have always been first priority. Dell was the first company in the industry to offer manufacturer-direct toll-free, 24-hour technical support service and next-day, on-site service programs that have become industry standards. (Roger A. Kerin and Robert A. Peterson, *Strategic Marketing Problems*, Englewood Cliffs: Prentice Hall, 1995, page 548)

Think of how a good auto dealer provides after-sales service (it's the reason Andi is on her third Honda in 17 years!) or how L.L. Bean and Nordstrom handle customer returns. Model your business on theirs.

To ask the hard question is simple.

W. H. AUDEN

What kind of sales training do you provide? Salespeople aren't born knowing how to sell, and although you may provide them with reams of information on your product or service, sales is an art that needs to be taught. The Small Business Administration's SCORE (Service Corps of Retired Executives) and SBDC (Small Business Development Center) programs, as well as those at local colleges or through your chamber of commerce, provide excellent workshops on sales. Sales training is one of the best investments you can make in your company. It has a fast payback, improves your staff's morale, and puts money in your pocket. What more could you ask for?

Training is everything. The peach was once a bitter almond; cauliflower is nothing but cabbage with a college education.

MARK TWAIN

Instead of having sales employees, you might consider using independent sales representatives. The advantages are that they're pros at selling and can keep your overhead costs lower. You can set them up through the entire country or just in selected markets. They are paid on a commission basis.

Since good reps are invaluable and bad ones a disaster, keep these points in mind. First and foremost, make sure the products they represent are compatible with yours. Provide the rep with good sales training aids and copies of your brochures to leave with prospective customers. Most important, don't sever ties with your customers just because you work with reps. Some of the after-order servicing is usually best handled by you.

How do you find qualified reps to handle your line? National trade shows often have bulletin boards set up for rep contacts. But make your final selection only after you've had face-to-face meetings.

Last, but not least, is your sales presentation. A good one leaves a strong, positive image in the customer's memory and paves the way for future discussion. It's better to leave one strong visual image of the product's superior performance than to overwhelm the customer with a multimedia song and dance.

Make sure your presentation is adapted to your audience. Know your customers and know their needs. A canned sales presentation can alienate an audience and indicate your lack of training and skills.

Don't scrimp on sales literature that you plan to leave behind. It should "look good" and reinforce the product's advantages that differentiate it from those of your competitors' products.

Merck and other leading drug companies spend over a year training their college-educated sales recruits and they often prefer to hire pharmacy majors. That's because their sales forces are interacting with doctors who must be expert in their judgments about what to prescribe to patients. (Peter R. Dickson, *Marketing Management*, Fort Worth: The Dryden Press, 1994, page 385)

The guarantee of continuity is quality.

EDDIE RICKENBACKER

SECTION 4:

Interacting with Your Customers

12

How Do You Prospect for More Customers?

The notion of prospecting reminds us of the '49ers and the Klondike gold rush. Remember Robert Service's poem "The Cremation of Sam Magee"? "Strange things are done 'neath the midnight sun by the men who moil for gold, and the Northern Lights have seen strange sights that would make your blood run cold. . . ."

Prospectors spent most of their time trying to separate gold from gravel. The most common method for small operators was to scoop up some gravel from the bottom of a stream with a pan, then slosh water about hoping to wash away the lighter material and capture a small amount of gold dust—or better yet, a nugget. Bigger operators spent more time up front building sluiceways so they could divert the cold water over a screen and thus try out larger amounts of gravel.

This kind of prospecting was cold, hard, discouraging work driven by hope of profit.

Commercial prospecting is the same. Maybe the conditions you prospect in are better and less hazardous, but you still have to moil for gold. (The dictionary defines "moil" as drudgery, hard work, derived from an archaic verb meaning "to moisten.")

When you prospect for new customers be prepared to moil as you separate real customers from the others who would take up your time. Nobody ever claimed that prospecting was easy.

When Andi and her business partner Janet Taylor published a weekly arts-and-entertainment paper in Portsmouth, New Hampshire, called *re:Ports.*, they were constantly on the lookout for more advertisers. As a free publication, advertising revenue was the lifeblood of *re:Ports.'* business. Janet and Andi would focus their sales efforts on certain towns or types of businesses each week, depending on the editorial focus of the upcoming issues. They made cold calls, both in person and on the phone, and spent lots of time and effort cultivating new customers. As new owners of the business, they saw their sales efforts as public relations efforts as well. They had the opportunity to meet current and prospective advertisers face to face, and thank them for their support.

If hard work were such a wonderful thing, surely the rich would have kept it all to themselves.

LANE KIRKLAND

Prospecting could be defined as a process of disqualification: You start with a sense of who might purchase your wares, then selectively weed out those persons who won't (or most likely won't) become customers.

This saves time. You will find fairly soon that large chunks of your widest market can be disqualified. This first cut is important to do in order to save time and effort. If you see other groups that can be disqualified, go to it. You will only make your lists more valuable.

Then apply the golden rule of prospecting: qualify, qualify, qualify. A qualified prospect is much more valuable to you than any number of unqualified prospects. They are closer to making a purchasing decision, have authority or at least influence to sign or authorize a check, and so on. Depending on your markets, your qualification process will be different—but it will always revolve around qualifying your prospects before trying to spur them to action.

Murray Raphel, a legendary Atlantic City merchant, said that the secret of successful prospecting has four parts. He called this his "Four-Plan."

Give four new people your business card every day. Assuming that your card is a good one (useful, informative, sufficiently interesting to be read), it doesn't matter whom you give them to. He gave them to waiters, cab drivers, business acquaintances, friends, anyone with whom he came in touch.

Write and send four notes or personal letters, handwritten for greater personality, to prospects every day. This adds up to over 2,000 contacts per year.

Make four phone calls to prospects every day. Again, this adds up. If nothing else it keeps you in touch with an ever-widening circle.

Ask for four referrals to put on your prospect list. This will keep your list fresh.

The big secret, Murray adds, is to do this consistently, day in and day out, no matter what else you have to do. Don't just do it when you think it'd be fun or agreeable.

Hide not your Talents, they for Use were made. What's a Sun-Dial in the Shade?

Poor Richard's Almanac

Attend your prospects' trade shows. You can't find a better prospecting arena. Although the initial cost of attending trade shows may seem steep, keep in mind that the average sales call costs more than $600 these days. At the trade shows, you get to chat up dozens of prospects, case the competition, see what's hot and what's not, and as a bonus get brought up to date on the latest industry gossip. Not a bad return on your investment!

If you can, get on one of the many panels that such shows provide. Both of us have run programs and know how difficult it is to get speakers and panelists who know what they are talking about and can present well. Hone your skills; become a welcome expert. Though you may not get on the agenda the first few

When Andy's cousin Jim Dickerson found himself out of a job (he'd been a bank president, a tough job to follow), JD decided to aggressively network to find new job prospects. JD would meet with at least four new people every day and try to get at least four referrals from each one. His results were more than satisfactory. JD wanted to get out of administration and back into a more hands-on position. He thought that fund-raising would be most rewarding (his father had been a fund-raiser for a private college), and added private banking and investment counseling as possibilities. He says he soon found out a lot more about these fields and as a bonus got to meet hundreds of interesting people. After nearly a year, JD found his ideal position—as a private banker for one of the largest banks in the world, a job he finds challenging, lucrative, and never dull.

times you try, keep at it. These shows can turn you into a prospect magnet.

What you don't ask for, you don't get.
AMERICAN PROVERB

Your former customers are a surprisingly fruitful source of new leads—and maybe more important, of new insights into how your products or services are perceived by your customers. After all, they wouldn't be former customers unless they had some reason to change. (Well, they may have moved out of your trading area, have different needs these days, and so on. True.)

Have you tried revisiting your former customers?

Cold calling is a time-honored prospecting technique. Admittedly, this isn't something most of us enjoy, but there are ways to take the sting out of it.

Go in with reasonable expectations. You aren't here to make a sale. Your goal is to make new friends, lay the groundwork for a future appointment, and gain information.

Treat cold calls as simply information gathering. You want to know what competing products they use, how happy they are with those products, who the players are, and so forth. You aren't selling. Prospecting is looking for people who may become customers some other time.

Use referrals whenever possible. They open doors for you, and if you don't abuse the referrals, tend to be excellent long-term sources of leads.

Do your homework. Cold calls don't have to be blind calls. What is the company? Look them up in Thomas's Register. Visit their Web site. Peer at their annual or quarterly reports. The more you know before the call, the more you'll learn from it.

Make friends with the gatekeeper, usually a receptionist whose main job is keeping his or her boss from being interrupted. He or she can be a great ally.

Make cold calling a habit. After a while, it won't be so frightening.

Smile and dial for prospects. There are a lot of books and tapes on this topic. Amazon.com lists 27 bestsellers! These books can help you with the mechanics of making prospecting calls, writing effective scripts, and learning how to respond to questions and stalls.

Use a good telephone list, "good" being a list with persons who are at least partially qualified. A raw list of random consumers will just eat up your time and phoning dollars.

You need a script. Winging it leads nowhere. You can always adapt your script as experience dictates, but without one it is very easy to forget a major point.

Your script should help you *briefly* introduce yourself and your reason for making the call. This is not unlike cold calling in that you are looking for information, for qualified prospects whom you will follow up on later.

Practice your script before making any calls. That makes the script familiar enough to you so you won't come across as presenting a canned spiel.

This may sound funny, but smile as you talk, even when practicing. It isn't called "smiling and dialing" just because it rhymes. It is called that because it

Shortly after Andi went to work as an editor for Andy's publishing company, Upstart, in 1982, he sent her off to the Bank Marketing Association's annual trade show in Dallas. Her mission? Gather as much information as possible on the competition (other providers of newsletters to banks), many of whom had booths at the show, and talk to as many bankers as possible, to find out what their marketing objectives were and what kinds of products they were looking for. She returned with lots of valuable information on the competition and many new contacts for prospective clients.

In her first year as a Nu Skin (a Provo, Utah-based cosmetics and natural products manufacturer that sells its products through network marketing) distributor, Barbara Casey Freundt made a list of 200 people and signed up 30 new distributors. In her second year, she had 1,000 people in her down-line, with total sales of $3 million. As a mother of six, she says that women raising children have mastered a sophisticated skill set that includes networking. "Mothers network constantly," she said, "seeking out the resources they need for their children—the best school, the best piano teacher, the most family-friendly vacation spot." (*Working at Home*, Winter 1998, page 104)

affects the tone of your voice—a smile wins more friends than a terrified grimace.

If someone is rude, caustic, hangs up, or simply is not interested, *your call is a successful one*. You have picked up some valuable information, culled your list a bit, and disqualified a name. That's good progress.

Think of dividing your lists (after calling) into three parts:

- A-list: These are your most qualified names; follow up very soon.
- B-list: Save these names for a call in three months; they may be qualified by then.
- C-list: If you think of prospecting as cherry picking, these guys are the pits; spit 'em out.

Networking is another great prospecting tactic, especially if you carefully choose a venue with prequalified prospects. This is why business mixers are so popular. Trade shows and seminars are also hotbeds.

Keep in mind that prospecting is not selling; rather it is a careful screening of people in your target market. Don't forget that some folks who will never buy your goods or services are important: Some people act as referrers, as influences on other people who will actually become your hottest prospects.

About all you can expect from networking is to generate a list of people to call or talk or write to later. By not selling but being an active and interested listener instead, your payoff will be greater if somewhat postponed. People love good listeners!

The same applies at trade shows. Don't sell. Listen, suggest, capture names (use their business cards and scribble brief reminders on the back of the cards)—and follow up promptly after the show.

He who desires but acts not, breeds pestilence.
WILLIAM BLAKE

Volunteer work is closely related to networking but more powerful. Be an active board member of a nonprofit, and you will get to be known as a concerned citizen, show what you can do (not just talk about it), and meet some fascinating and influential people.

Both of us are active this way, not necessarily to generate a reputation but to serve causes in which we believe. Andi is very active in the New Hampshire Writer's Project, and does volunteer work for other arts and political organizations and her synagogue. Andy is a founding director of the New Hampshire Women's Business Center (and permanent secretary), active on several nonprofit economic development boards, on the executive board of a graduate school of business, and in his spare time on the vestry of his church. (Whew!)

As we quoted Theodore Levitt earlier in this book, it isn't whom you know but how you are known to them. Volunteer service gives you an unbeatable platform to show what you can do.

From what we get, we can make a living;
what we give, however, makes a life.
ARTHUR ASHE

Volunteerism can help raise the productivity of a work force, and reduce absenteeism and office stress. A study by the Independent Sector, a philanthropic research and information group, cites the following benefits of volunteerism to employees: "allows me to gain a new perspective on things" (78 percent); "makes me feel needed" (68 percent); "helps me deal with some of my personal problems" (40 percent); "provides me with new contacts that help me with my business or career" (23 percent). Chase Manhattan Bank has a terrific volunteer program called Global Days of Service. In 1998, it connected more than 10,000 employees to a spectrum of volunteer activities. To help match workers with nonprofit organizations, Johnson & Johnson hires college interns to set up a clearinghouse. (Peter Lynch, "Lost Time," *Worth*, June 1999)

Our favorite investment banker, Pete Worrell, uses a clipping service to provide the raw material that he then sends along to his extensive list of friends, prospects, and customers. He makes the call on who gets sent what—that's the personal touch, a sine qua non for effective prospecting in his field. Lots of people have the technical skills. Very few have the people skills, and this little considerate activity is just one of the many manifestations of his ability to communicate effectively, briefly, and helpfully.

Some people use clipping services as a fast way to keep up with personnel changes in an industry. A short congratulatory note on a promotion, even from a stranger, is welcome.

You can use a clipping service to spot industry trends, and that in turn will lead you to new sets of prospects.

Think of the clipping service as a way to save time, generate a great deal of industry-specific information, and find business opportunities that might otherwise elude you.

Always do right—this will gratify some and astonish the rest.

MARK TWAIN

According to some of our friends, you are only five people away from anyone on Earth that you might possibly wish to meet. Though this may be a bit unrealistic, you will find that asking for referrals pays off fast.

Don't be afraid to ask for referrals. Ask for names of people who might be interested in what you have to sell. Murray Raphel used to claim that the magic phrase is: "I have a problem. Could you help me?" As he points out, the worst that happens is that the person says no.

More likely, he or she will feel flattered to be asked, and unless there is a good reason to deny your request for names and referrals, you'll come away with some prospects you'd never find any other way.

A gentle word opens an iron gate.

BULGARIAN PROVERB

Reading and observation pay off. What are you looking for? Names—lots of names, ideally, of prequalified prospects who you hope to convert to customers. Trade publications and shows are sources of lists. So are mail-order lists, which can be rented for testing against your selection criteria. Magazines rent their lists. Andy gets flooded with boat-related offers because he subscribes to boating magazines like Wooden Boat and Cruising World. Andi finds her mailbox full of seed catalogs (she collects them) and offers for gourmet cooking equipment.

How did our names get on these lists? We both have a record of buying things from catalogs (excellent, says the marketer) and have easily discerned interests (goody, the marketer cries). We have been qualified in other words. Our names have value. Some lists are worth several dollars per name because they contain all and only qualified buyers.

We are all on someone's list. Can you find one that meets your prequalification criteria?

Better is the enemy of good.

FRANCOIS VOLTAIRE

Use a contact management system to handle your prospect lists. Andy uses one called Act! A contact list helps you sort out the names according to category, set tickler files to make sure you send a note or make a call or meet for lunch, keep an accurate activity record for each prospect, and even dial the right number (assuming you enter it correctly in the first place).

Referrals are the most effective techniques for attracting new customers, according to a survey conducted by the Nierenberg Group in New York City. The 900 sales and marketing professionals agreed that "the shortest path to new customers comes from reviewing existing contracts and asking them who might give you the warmest reception." (*Inc.*, July 1999, page 93)

The competition to win a place on the mailing lists of elite West Coast wineries is not a sport but a frenzy. Obsessive and affluent oenophiles, bored by the wine at their local liquor stores, crave hard-to-get vintages available only in a few pricey restaurants and sold to individuals exclusively through the mail. But customers who "cherry pick" offerings, misplace order forms, or get their orders in later than others are often relegated to the waiting list. "If we send you a mailer and you don't buy anything, your name drops to the waiting list," says a spokesperson at Turley Wine Cellars. (*Worth*, "Wait Listed Again," October 1998)

If your list is more than 50 names long, you need a contact manager. They are an inexpensive way to manage the information that drives the qualification process, can cost as little as $50 for a good shareware program or as much as several hundred dollars for a more powerful system.

Check a few out. You'll be glad you did.

13

How Do You Keep Customers Coming Back?

The relationship between you and your customers doesn't end when a sale is made. If anything, it gets more involved—particularly if you're a vendor or consultant, or in the financial services, general contracting, or capital goods industries. Since your customers will probably need to buy your product or service again, it's your responsibility to make sure they return to you—a second time, a third, a fourth, and more.

How do you keep your customers coming back? There are three bases that must always be covered. First you make it easy for them to buy from you. Second, you stand behind your product/service and the promises you make. And third, you keep channels of communication open. You take the initiative for staying in touch by writing a note, picking up the phone, forwarding helpful information, and always finding some way to show your appreciation for your customers' business.

The relationship between you and your customers is like a marriage. If a customer feels you're strongly committed to the relationship, as when you go the extra mile in your after-sales service or address a problem promptly, he or she won't be so quick to jump to the competitor's ship when a problem arises—even if its a doozy. Customers are loyal to businesses that show them dedication and commitment over the long haul.

> Gillette North America has four separate sales forces. There are special programs for major accounts designed to assure Gillette's rapid response to their needs. In addition, there's a vice president of business relations who has among his major duties, separate from the sales organization, the cultivation of Gillette's relationships with major retailers and distributors via a vast array of ceremonial activities. They range from hosting cocktail parties, dinners and entertainments at 12 annual trade association conventions, to the organization of special events for major accounts in connection with the World Series and the Super Bowl, to attending charitable dinners and retirement parties for presidents of major retail chains. (Theodore Levitt, *The Marketing Imagination*, New York: The Free Press, 1983, page 122)

But if customer service sours and communication withers on the vine, divorce is the likely upshot.

Remember that your company's most precious asset is its relationships with its customers. Nurture them with care and respect, and chances are those relationships will last a long time.

The sweetest grapes hang the highest.

GERMAN PROVERB

How do you sustain relationships with your customers through thick and thin? You begin by understanding their needs and tailoring your after-sale services accordingly.

For example, as busy dog owners, we really appreciate the postcard reminders we get from our vets notifying us of our dogs' needs for shots and exams. Our vets keep us on schedule and our dogs healthy, and show us that they really care about our pets' well-being. Andi wishes her own doctor would remind her to schedule yearly checkups!

What matters to your customers? The reminders you send for appointments? The hours you're open for business? Your staff's friendliness? Your technicians' expertise and courtesy? The consistency of your product line? Your ability to customize products or services to a client's individual needs? Your standing as a leader in your field or in your community? To find out, take a survey, either formally or informally.

As we said earlier, talk with and listen to your customers. You'll learn a lot that will help you serve them better and ultimately make your business more profitable.

More than cleverness,
we need kindness and gentleness.
CHARLIE CHAPLIN, THE GREAT DICTATOR

No matter what industry it's in, every business is a service business when it comes to customers. Part of every business' mission is to make it easy for customers to buy from them—again and again.

If you went through the exercises we suggested in Chapter 5, then you know who your customers are and what they want from you. Review your records to see how many repeat customers you have and how long they've been with you. The rule of thumb is that it costs five times more to gain a new customer than it does to retain an existing one. That's powerful financial incentive to keep customers returning to you.

Forsake not an old friend; for the new is not comparable to him: a new friend is as new wine; when it is old, thou shalt drink it with pleasure.
ECCLESIASTES, 9:10

Your front-line staff is your most valuable asset when it comes to customer service.

Make sure you've hired the right people—ones with excellent interpersonal skills who can think on their feet. Pay them fairly for their skills and empower

The best-known example of an industry-wide study of customer satisfaction is the J.D. Power and Associates Customer Satisfaction Index for automakers. Each March the company (which also offers surveys to computer manufacturers) sends out a six-page survey to some 70,000 owners of new cars. About one-third respond. Manufacturers receive detailed reports of problem areas and benchmark comparisons with their competitors. Customer handling (before- and after-sales service from the dealer) has accounted for more than 40 percent of the score, and J.D. Power's influence on auto dealers has grown extraordinarily since the service began in the early 1980s. (Peter R. Dickson, *Marketing Management*, Fort Worth: The Dryden Press, 1994, page 572)

Honda was the first to use J.D. Powers's satisfaction ratings in a very effective advertising campaign, and other companies have followed suit. As a loyal Honda owner for the past 16 years, Andi can attest to the impeccable customer service of her dealer, Dover Auto Center in Dover, New Hampshire. It offers the best and most trustworthy mechanics on the planet, courteous and friendly staff at the service desk who know her when she calls for appointments—and have made special accommodations for her during emergencies (only 2 in 17 years—a stellar record!), and makes follow-up calls to customers after every appointment. The price of this service? Well, it may be high and it may not. Andi hates to admit that she has not even bothered to compare prices because she wouldn't feel secure or comfortable taking her business anywhere else.

them to do whatever is necessary to make your customers happy. Allow them to offer refunds, swap products, or provide free consulting services.

Empowering your employees means backing up their decisions—even if they happen to make a wrong one. Despite the best and most thorough customer-service training, employees encounter situations that no one could possibly have foreseen. Assuming you've hired the right people, you must then conclude that they'll make the best decisions possible when crises confront them. If a staffer makes a mistake, explain what you expect instead and then move on. What really counts is whether your customers feel that their complaints were handled well, and whether they'll return to you, rather than to your competitor, the next time they need your product or service.

Return customers are worth their weight in gold. Remember Pareto's rule: 80 percent of your business comes from 20 percent of your customers. The secret to your success in business is keeping those 20 percent happy and returning again and again.

In addition to hiring "people" people for your front-line positions, there are many other ways you can reinforce customer-service values throughout your company. Think of the Golden Rule: Do unto others as you would have them do unto you. Always treat people fairly and with respect, and you'll never go wrong.

One of the easiest ways to show respect is to return phone calls and e-mails quickly. Even if you don't have an answer to a customer's question, let him or her know you're in the process of finding one. As a customer, nothing's worse than feeling that your concerns aren't a priority.

Take the time to personally make a delivery—when there's no looming deadline or crisis. Not only is it a chance to show your customers how much you value their business. It's also an opportunity to visit them on-site, where your product is used, and solicit some valuable feedback. Maybe they'll have an idea for improving your product or for a new product altogether. Chances are that if it meets their needs, it might meet the needs for many others like them.

There can be no defense like elaborate courtesy.
E. V. (EDWARD VERRALL) LUCAS

If your business depends on across-the-transom sales, make sure you're conveniently located, that there's adequate parking nearby, and you keep hours that are convenient for your customers. As consumers, we all know how frustrating it can be for stores to close at 5 pm on weekdays, just when we're getting off work, or for there to be nowhere to park after we've made an effort to get somewhere, or to be unable to find the office or store altogether. Proper signage, maps, and even validated parking are customer-service perks that can set your business apart from those of your competitors.

Customers also make judgments about service quality based on nonservice factors. Is your office or store clean, well-lit, and nicely furnished? Are your

Despite strong competition from the recent entry of big home-improvement chains in New England, independent garden centers have continued to survive, and even flourish. Local, family-owned independents have been able to capitalize on their strong ties to their communities, their broader selections of plants, and their knowledgeable sales staffs. At Mahoney's, a family-run chain of garden centers in Massachusetts, customer Stan Wheeler says, "Mahoney's is an outstanding name. The service you get here is worth the difference in price." (*The Boston Globe*, May 8, 1999, F-1)

No matter which McDonald's you visit—around the corner from where you work, in Japan, or anywhere in between—you know that your cheeseburger and fries are going to taste the same, that the restaurant will open early and serve breakfast, that your meal will be inexpensive, and that the bathrooms will be clean. That consistency brings happy customers back again and again—not only do they know what to expect, but they're also certain that those expectations will be met. To help satisfy customers' appetites when they're away from home, McDonald's Corp.'s Web site, *www.mcdonalds.com* has added a trip planner that locates its restaurants and estimates mileage and driving time to reach them along a vacation or travel route. The company says customers often call to map out on-the-road locations.

printed materials (letterhead, business cards, invoices, ads, and so on) good looking and of high quality? Is your staff appropriately attired?

A good way to test the quality of customer service in your establishment is to hire phantom shoppers. Pay people to call your company or shop in your store or eat in your restaurant, and evaluate the way your front-line staff handles customers. Or you can regularly call a few randomly selected customers and simply ask about the company's service.

Happiness is a warm puppy.

Charles Schulz

Despite any business owner's best intentions, life is full of unexpected problems occurring at inopportune times, and everyone has his or her war stories. But no matter what inconveniences a customer might encounter, what makes him or her loyal to a particular business is how he or she is treated. If customers' concerns are a priority, if phone calls are promptly returned, if a business's return policy is liberal, if a company guarantees its work, if communication is excellent, and if loaners or replacements are readily available, a customer will be satisfied that everything is being done to resolve his or her problem no matter how serious it might be. If customers feel that they're treated royally, they'll return when they need to buy again. That loyalty is worth its weight in gold.

Keep in mind that 68 percent of customers who take their business elsewhere do so because they believe that the company couldn't care less if they remain a customer, according to the Technical Assistance Research Programs, Inc., a Washington, D.C.-based consulting firm. Don't ever let your customers think that their loyalty is wasted on you!

I have more care to stay than will to go.
WILLIAM SHAKESPEARE, ROMEO AND JULIET

One way to head off problems at the pass is to make follow-up phone calls immediately after sales are completed. Ask your customers whether the product or service meets their specifications and whether they're satisfied. Ask how they interacted with the salesperson and other staff in your company. Also ask if anything could be improved so that their experience buying from you could be even more pleasant, more efficient, more convenient. Constantly solicit feedback and use it to improve your business.

Another way to avoid problems is to make realistic promises, whether they concern delivery dates, product longevity, or product/service features. If you include a benefit in a product name or tag line, you better deliver. Jolt Cola had better give you an energy boost, and the Big Mac had better satisfy a big appetite.

Amazon.com's CEO Jeff Bezos credits the company's success to a deceptively simple goal: He wants it to be the most customer-focused company ever—both online and off. That's why Amazon has spent heavily to build several distribution centers around the world to hasten deliveries. And that's why the company has spent countless hours tweaking its Web pages to remove every possible obstacle to purchasing. It invented one-click ordering, which lets buyers store credit cards and addresses after the first purchase, and it installed software that assesses what people have bought and suggests other purchases. The result: Repeat purchasers account for 66 percent of sales. (*Business Week*, "eBay Vs. Amazon.com," May 25, 1999)

"We may have stopped advertising, but we haven't stopped communicating," says Amy Brinkmoeller, director of information systems at Dorothy Lane Markets, a $38 million operator of two upscale groceries in Dayton Ohio. Brinkmoeller, who's in charge of the loyalty program, sends out a monthly newsletter to the company's top 9,000 customers. The company decided to break rank with competitors and discontinue newspaper advertising in an effort to weed out all the people who weren't regular customers. The result: the most radical loyalty program in the supermarket industry and an extra three points of gross margin to give back to its best customers. The newsletters have different versions with coupons pegged to different spending levels. Four to six customized communications go out, usually in postcard form, every month. The loyalty program has allowed CEO Norman Mayne to focus more on his customers and less on his competition. (*Fast Company*, June 1999, page 76)

Ask, and it shall be given you; seek, and ye shall find; knock, and it shall be opened unto you.

ST. MATTHEW

Communication is the cornerstone of customer service. In addition to soliciting feedback from your customers, never forget to thank them for their business. You can do this with a telephone call, a personal visit, an invitation to lunch, a bouquet of flowers, a special gift, or a handwritten thank-you note.

Keep your customers apprised of special events, and let them know that because of their status as special customers, they're hearing in advance of the general public. Recognize customers' one-, five- and ten-year anniversaries for doing business with your company by sending a card or special gift. Let them know that their business means the world to you.

Always thank a customer for a referral—in a timely fashion. Pick up the phone, send flowers, or take a few minutes to handwrite a thank-you note.

In most of mankind gratitude is merely a secret hope of further favors.

FRANCOIS LA ROCHEFOUCAULD

The trick to not losing customers or having to win back disgruntled ones is picking the right ones in the first place. Know who your core customers are, those 20 percent who are responsible for 80 percent of your business, and serve them well. By the same token, know who your marginal customers are and don't spend too much time on them. With limited time and resources, you need to make sure both are profitably spent.

Looking at small advantages prevents great affairs from being accomplished.

CONFUCIUS

In an effort to win back investors upset by poor returns and fund manager defections, Fidelity Investments launched a charm offensive. It invited 5,300 clients, each with at least $1 million in their Fidelity accounts, to 13 hotels in 10 cities to watch a live discussion among top portfolio managers about investing and Fidelity. "It's a way to educate the consumer and keep in touch with customers," says Fidelity spokesperson Thomas Edison. Around 80 percent of Fidelity's business comes from its top 20 percent customers. James Lowell, editor of the independent *Fidelity Investor* newsletter, said, "Fidelity has learned a valuable lesson with its road show—investors love contact with money managers." (*The Boston Globe*, May 12, 1999, D-6)

14

Does E-commerce Make Sense for Your Business?

The Internet is a vast collection of more than 60,000 inter-connected networks that all use the TCP/IP (Transmission Control Protocol/Internet Protocol) to facilitate the transmission of data from one network to another. The jargon of the Internet is daunting, so you may want to go to the ILC Glossary of Internet Terms at *www.matisse.net/files/glossary/html* to get an updated list of definitions. What matters to you as a business owner is that the Internet gives you access to a practically unlimited amount of information, people and markets, and business opportunities. All you need is a computer, a modem, and a browser such as Netscape. Both of us use America Online as our server (it provides a wide range of services made simple for those of us who are electronically challenged) but would probably not use it for e-commerce.

You can access the Electronic Commerce Resource Center at the University of Scranton to get a quick overview of the Internet and the possibilities of e-commerce. Their URL (Uniform Resource Locator, or World Wide Web address) is *www.ecrc.uofs.edu.*

Some of the most useful services on the Internet include:

- *E-mail* (electronic mail) to send messages to one or more persons via computer. The message can be as complex as you can imagine, contain pictures, text, sound, executable software, and lots more;

"E-business 2.0 seen as path for on-line success: Running of sites to shift towards marketing people," reads the headline in the *Portsmouth Herald*, September 28, 1999. E-business 1.0 was about developing Web sites to market and promote products to local markets. E-business 2.0 is about taking orders and payments for goods and services globally. "Where the traditional company did things in weeks, e-businesses do them in minutes or even seconds. Where product design was traditionally done by the company, in e-business it was often done by the customers: Instead of standard products, they wanted customized ones. Instead of production being pre-sales, in e-business it was often post-sales. And instead of location being the strategic driver (traditionally, customers buy locally), an e-business strategy must be based on service."

- *WWW*, or the World Wide Web (sometimes called simply the Web);
- *Search engines* such as Gopher, Yahoo!, Alta Vista, Ask Jeeves, and so on are databases that help you find information on the Web. Veronica is a database of Gopher databases. Since the information is very widely dispersed, you need to master the use of more than one search engine.
- *Web sites or home pages* have to reside in a directory that is accessible by a Web server program to be "on the Web."

See why you'll need a glossary? (Actually it's pretty simple once you take the time to surf the Web and see how things work.)

E-business is more than just selling things on-line. It is about changing the ways companies work.
MICHAEL DELL, FOUNDER OF DELL COMPUTER

Technically, e-commerce is a cover term for all electronic commerce modes, which would include telephone, fax, pager, computer based, and any other commerce based, on electronic media. The term "Internet commerce" (or I-commerce) hasn't taken hold in the public usage, so e-commerce has come to be associated with this limited part of electronic commerce.

The buzz is that e-commerce is going to take over an ever-increasing share of the marketplace. Web marketing is just a piece of e-commerce, and as more and more business is done on the Internet, more and more resources will have to be devoted to Web marketing.

The longer I live the more keenly I feel that whatever was good enough for our fathers is not good enough for us.

OSCAR WILDE

The benefits of e-commerce are just beginning to be realized. As with any fast growing market, there's a "boom-town" aspect to it, sort of an electronic wild, wild West where fortunes are made (and lost) practically overnight. Aside from the highly publicized success of Netscape, Amazon, American Online, e-Bay, and other pioneers, and the rapid entry of well-established brick-and-mortar companies like Barnes & Noble, the main growth is coming from the thousands of small- and medium-sized businesses all over the world who are discovering new ways of making money on the Internet.

You can market globally, not just locally. Suppose you have a phenomenal Grand Marnier chocolate sauce like Andi's. You could sell it traditionally door-to-door or in local markets. You could sell it in a catalog (if you can get accepted by, say, Williams Sonoma). Or—and this is where it becomes exciting—you could sell it all over the world, cost-effectively, using a Web site to promote it, including different recipes and uses of the sauce, making a personal connection with the customers, collecting information on visitors to your Web site, and providing interactive, fast communication. Not a bad idea!

Seven Ways to Use the Internet

1. Do research.
2. Provide information.
3. Provide discussion forums.
4. Provide training.
5. Provide on-line buying and selling.
6. Provide on-line auctioning or exchanging.
7. Provide on-line "bits" delivery.

(Phillip Kotler, *Kotler on Marketing*, Englewood Cliffs: Prentice Hall, 1999, page 217)

Autobytel.com, one of the United States' leading car-buying sites, plans a major push into Western Europe in a bid to stay ahead of its on-line rivals. While it faces stiff competition at home from companies such as Autoweb.com, Microsoft's Carpoint, and Classified Ventures' cars.com, the firm sees Western Europe as a largely untapped market. And demand for services there might be greater, since the European market is about equal to the size of that in the U.S. Autobytel.com's first task, however, appears to be educating Europeans about the benefits of buying on-line. (*The Wall Street Journal*, September 27, 1999, B-19E)

One of the best things about e-commerce is that it provides measurable results. How many people visit your Web site? How many buy something? How many ask for information, referrals, links to other similar sites? This valuable and measurable interactivity is hard to get through normal marketing channels. A well-designed Web site can gather this information for you.

The Internet has become the ultimate medium for business.
LOUIS V. GERSTNER JR., CEO OF IBM

The advantages of e-commerce for small business are many. Here are a few:

Costs are low and controllable. While a Web site can cost millions of dollars it doesn't have to be expensive. It's a lot less expensive to change the specs of a product or change a price on your Web site than to reprint and mail brochures.

You can control inventory costs: The customer orders, you ship. Since the pattern is measurable you can decide what level of inventory to stock. Not incidentally, this is Dell Computer's competitive advantage over competitors who maintain traditional business practices.

You can target tight markets worldwide. You can search (at a very low cost) for growth markets, the ones where you can ideally ride a set market share to riches. Why limit yourself to local markets when you can (if you can) access national or global markets? It is as easy to sell your chocolate sauce to someone in Shanghai as in your own town. Maybe easier.

You can help your customers satisfy themselves. What brand, flavor, style do they want? How do they want to be billed? You have more flexibility than you may imagine.

You can easily monitor your competitors on the Web. What works for them? What doesn't work? Can you do it better, improve it by using your wits, or provide better service? Your Web site is open 24 hours a day, 7 days a week. Delivery services can take over the routine distribution chores.

All of us want to sell toast, not toasters; quarter inch holes, not drill bits. The Internet provides a means for you to find out what kind of toast or quarter-inch hole your markets want.

We hasten to add that this brief list just scratches the surface of benefits. The Web is a dynamic, exciting new business venue in which new benefits are created daily.

Staples, Inc., has launched a new ad campaign to help drive traffic to its retail Web site at *www.staples.com*. The campaign features a TV spot, along with radio, print, billboard, and on-line advertising. "Our goal is to be the preeminent office supply retailer to small business, whether they shop at staples.com, in our retail stores, or through our catalog," said Staples.com president Jeanne Lewis. "To do this, we need to market ourselves online and off-line to reach all our target customers." (*The Boston Globe*, September 24, 1999, E-3)

Fanaticism consists in redoubling your effort when you have forgotten your aim.

GEORGE SANTAYANA

Naturally there are dangers inherent in a new enterprise. All of the usual dangers of commerce (competition, changes in markets, difficulty in cutting through the advertising clutter, cost control problems, and so on) exist in e-commerce.

Add to those these new problems:

Security considerations: How secure are electronic transactions? The public is being educated in this but, as with any missionary effort, it will take time for most people to be persuaded that e-commerce transactions, properly secured with existing technologies, is actually as safe as buying with cash and less dangerous than using a credit card in a restaurant. It is still a concern that you must address.

You have to set up a "firewall" between your computer and the Internet. Hackers like the challenge of breaking into someone else's computer from a distance, and can then wreak all sorts of problems once they gain entry. There are methods to minimize this danger, but they have to be built in to your systems early.

You will need virus protection to make sure you don't accidentally accept a problem along with an order.

State governments are increasingly eager to tax sales made on the Web, despite the federal government's support of the Internet and e-commerce. These tax issues are not going to go away. Imagine the difficulty of paying sales taxes in dozens of states and countries!

E-commerce is not right for every business. It looks appealing, and it is exciting—but not all businesses will be able to use it. There are hidden costs (technological, managerial, staffing) that can overwhelm you if you are not aware of them.

Opportunity costs cut both ways. You can waste a lot of time and effort trying to make sense of e-commerce. You could also miss the boat completely if you don't at least investigate the possibility that your business could use e-commerce. This is a big wave. A huge wave. You might ride it, might miss it, might get drowned by it. But you cannot ignore it.

Don't limit a child to your own learning,
for he was born in another time.
RABBINICAL SAYING

Competition is hot on the Web. Check out your competitors' Web sites. If one person has a bright idea today, by tomorrow (if not by this afternoon!) it will be copied. More important, you will see what other people are doing, how they do it, not just across the street but across the globe. Maybe you can pick up on a hot idea that works in Europe and put it to work in Colorado or Florida or wherever you live.

Remember that the reason to stay on top of your competition is not to imitate them (which is ultimately unsatisfactory anyway) but to learn from them. Your direct competitors come first, then the indirect (those who are trying to generate sales from your customers and prospects with different services or products), and finally the remote competitors, the new technology or idea that might impact your business. Go back to Chapter 6 to review the benefits of knowing all about your competitors.

You get out front—you stay out front.
RACE-CAR DRIVER A. J. FOYT

Use all of the elements of traditional marketing before embarking on e-commerce. E-commerce is not so different as it appears.

In 1996, Barbara and Bob Lefkowitz thought selling harmonicas to other music lovers over the Internet would be a fine symbiosis of a hobby and modest business ambitions. But soon, harmonica novices started calling to ask Barbara rudimentary questions on her 800 number, which was posted on the Web site. Others called to haggle over prices, especially if they saw a cheaper harmonica at a competitor's site. The low-margin business became too time-consuming, and the owners decided to close their Web site. (*The Wall Street Journal,* June 10, 1999, B-12)

You still have to ask what business you are in. Not all businesses benefit from e-commerce. Go back and review Chapter 1.

Can your product or service be sold on the Internet? Or does it require a personal demonstration? The jury is out on selling arts and crafts by e-commerce. Some items simply have to be picked up, looked over, smelled, tasted, or touched. The opportunity may be there for you. Or it may not.

What do you hope to accomplish with a Web site (if you decide to go forward, a Web site will be necessary)? Do you want to provide information, create sales leads, find new markets, explore offshore sales? Your goals still have to be measurable, believable, and achievable. The Web extends your reach. It doesn't absolve you from doing the grunt work of goal setting, researching, and carefully assessing results.

Finding potential customers, or prospecting, is one of the more exciting opportunities provided by the advent of e-commerce. But it takes research. What sites do your prospects visit, or are apt to visit? What else do they look for? You do just what you would with normal commerce: seek groups of people who can be identified, qualified, and accessed.

How you currently promote your goods and services has an impact on your decision about e-commerce. The Internet can be a profitable promotional opportunity for you.

Brochures and other printed matter can be adapted readily to this new medium. What differs is that the audience on the Internet has come to expect a higher level of sophistication and interactivity than print provides. They expect the information to be layered: They can choose the amount and depth of information to receive. They expect that it won't take very long to load on their screen. If they have to wait they leave, even if they are interested in your products.

Your URL (the address of your Web site) should be publicized in all your print media, including on your stationery, business cards, price lists, advertisements, brochures, newsletters, press releases, and whatever else you use. People may just stumble across your site while cruising the 'net, but that's inefficient and leaving too much to chance.

Make sure that your Web site designer includes links to all search engines under the metatags and key words that your prospects use to describe your goods and services. A good Web site designer will ask, much as a good advertising agent would— but there are plenty of tyro Web site designers out there who are more technically than marketing oriented.

Unlike printed material, Internet material can be kept fresh at very low cost. Your visitors don't want yesterday's information. They are impatient, increasingly wanting to access your material at their own pace rather than at yours. And they expect the information to be up-to-date.

We can't stress too strongly the importance of utilizing the dynamic nature of e-commerce. Look at Amazon.com for a good example of how to collect information on customer preferences. Andy gets notices of new sailing books. Andi gets notices about cookbooks and gardening. Amazon can tailor their promotions to individual tastes. How personal can you get?

Stamps.com is a three-year-old Santa Monica, California, company that allows consumers to buy postage online. Jeffrey Green, one of the three founders, is in a race—to establish partnerships with Quicken.com and AOL so that their customers will buy stamps from Green and not his competitors, and to prepare for the break-neck speed of growth his company has experienced. More than 100 employees have joined the company in three years. The company has moved five times, starting in an office for four people to now being in one that has more than 40,000 square feet of space. (*Entrepreneur*, September 1999, page 121)

In 1998 outdoor equipment retailer REI outfitted stores with kiosks so that customers could get product information and place orders on-line. Its cash registers have been upgraded so that cashiers can order merchandise from REI's Web site when it's not in stock at the store. By the end of 1999, the Web site is expected to be more profitable than any of the 55 stores. (*Business Week*, "No Web Site Is an Island," March 16, 1999)

Energy is Eternal Delight.
WILLIAM BLAKE

If you currently sell your goods and services only by traditional means, e-commerce will have some surprises for you. It will change the way you do business in profound ways.

Some businesses send CDs containing highly specialized ordering software to their major customers. This effectively marries the customer to the manufacturer or distributor—and makes it much easier for the purchaser to make the best decisions for his or her company. A few even make it possible to access competitors' sites. If you can't get a widget from us, you can get it from them. Think of the goodwill such service can generate.

Lead generation and processing can be handled in the office, leaving the sales force free to sell rather than perform (necessary) paperwork.

Even mundane parts and price lists can be changed on the fly, allowing great flexibility to the sales force.

Orders can be entered from the field, setting delivery dates that are realistic rather than optimistic. At the same time inventory requirements can be reduced.

Before leaping into e-commerce, carefully review all of the steps in your current sales process. You may find ways to improve them (we can almost guarantee that you will). By making these processes intentional you put yourself in a position to use the Internet to its fullest.

Let the great world spin for ever down the ringing grooves of change.
ALFRED TENNYSON

Target marketing is just as important in Web marketing as in traditional marketing, perhaps even more so.

Here is an example: iVillage.com has a Web site for women. If you are selling a product of interest to new mothers, iVillage has a site that they heavily promote to this target market.

Why is this important to know? Because you can buy advertising space (that's where iVillage makes its money) that will be seen by literally millions of prospects, who can then access your site with a single click of a mouse. Of course the ads are not cheap—but think of the value of having pre-qualified prospects going to your Web site, looking specifically for solutions to their problems that your product can provide.

These highly targeted sites are far more important to you than the general sites which, while useful for major consumer products such as Coca-Cola, are too broad for most smaller companies.

Where do you find these targeted sites? By doing some surfing of your own, going from one link to another. And by making sure to ask your customers how they use the Internet.

I am a great believer in luck and I find that the harder I work, the more I have of it.
STEPHEN LEACOCK

As companies large and small race to revamp operations for the Internet Age, they realize it's not enough to put up simple Web sites for customers, employees and partners. To take full advantage of the 'Net, they've got to reinvent the way they do business—changing how they distribute goods, collaborate inside the company and deal with suppliers. *Business Week* calls it "E-engineering" instead of reengineering. Drug giant Pfizer now dashes off electronic versions of its drug applications to the FDA in Washington, instead of trucking tons of paper to regulators. Pfizer's wired researchers now use the Web to mine libraries of technical data and collaborate on new drug development. At Intel Corporation, Web-based automation has liberated 200 salesclerks from tediously entering orders. Now, they concentrate on analyzing sales trends and pampering customers. (*Business Week*, "From Reengineering to E-Engineering," March 16, 1999)

Selling toys and other children's products on-line is expected to grow rapidly, because parents feel short of time and it is relatively simple to choose a toy over the Internet. Although Toys "Я" Us began selling on-line in June 1998, it was unable to catch up to eToys, Inc., an Internet-only retailer, because it hadn't treated its on-line sales effort as a separate unit. But with significant investment from venture-capital firm Benchmark Capital, Toys "Я" Us plans to create a new unit. The company believes its extensive sales network will actually help it sell more wares on-line. Shoppers will be able to avoid shipping costs by picking up toys at retail outlets, which also provide a convenient place to handle returns. (*The Wall Street Journal*, April 27, 1999, A-3)

E-commerce helps you find out what your customers want from you. It's a great research tool. A well-designed Web site will garner loads of insights for you if you include an interactive database in which your customers seek answers to questions pertinent to your goods or services. They ask. Your site provides answers, and at the same time captures and measures the levels of information being sought. As a general rule, the more they seek the closer they are to making a purchasing decision.

Can you get customers to give you their names and address (e-mail or other)? You sure can. Remember that they visit your Web site for one of three reasons: they surfed onto it by chance, sought it out, or came across it by keyword or metatag. If they stay they do so for only two reasons: They are charmed by the site, or they are really interested in what you have to offer them.

What is research but a blind date with knowledge?

WILL HENRY

Are you concerned about the price of your product? Here's a novel pricing technique: Put your product on a few of the auction sites (such as eBay.com) and see how it is really valued by the market.

You retain your customers in the real world by providing goods or services which meet their demands at a price which they find acceptable. No mystery there. You do the same in the electronic world. Deliver what you promised.

Andy's friend Ron Michaels worked as a consultant to companies like McDonald's and organizations like the University of Arizona. He taught Andy three "laws":

1. Marketing battles are never won. They are lost by failure to observe basic common-sense practices, usually because of complacency.
2. Give the customer more than they expect but not so much as to shock them. Customers value consistency. Ever visit a McDonald's that was dirty? Didn't think so.
3. Minimize opportunities for customer dissatisfaction.

E-commerce heeds these same laws. Failure to deliver as promised, or to keep the site updated (read: clean!), or to engage in sloppy thinking about what might be unsatisfactory for the customer all lead to failure.

Does this take work? Of course it does. We never promised that e-commerce would be easy!

How can you get started in e-commerce? Here are some initial suggested steps:

First, make sure that the Internet makes sense for your company. Are your competitors on the Web? Then you should probably be there, too.

Second, form a strategy. The core small business strategies of Focus, Personalize, Customize (or Specialize), and Simplify are a good guide.

What do you want to accomplish on the Web? Increased sales or profits? Heightened customer knowledge? Service to new markets?

Mainspring Inc., a Cambridge, Massachusetts, consulting company that specializes in e-commerce strategies, helped Scudder Kemper Investments relaunch its Web site. One of the strategic elements Mainspring helped with was electronic mail for customer feedback. "This customer feedback is guiding some of our decision in the design of the site," explained Scudder vice president Greg Titus. Mainspring also recommended the investment company's customer representatives be allowed to access personal financial profile information customers keep on the Scudder Web site so they can offer better and more informed service. (*The Boston Globe*, April 28, 1999, D-1)

How will e-commerce make your business better? Will it save money, cut inventories, speed up operations, ensure higher quality, help you grow?

How will e-commerce make your customers more satisfied? Will it make it easier for them to buy, help them understand the product or service better, make distribution easier?

Third, seek resources. The Electronic Commerce Resource Center, or ECRC *www.ecrc.uofs.edu,* is one of 18 technical centers scattered around the country. Colleges are increasingly involved in e-commerce. MIT's Sloan School of Management is about as prestigious an institution as you could wish—and they have just started a concentration in e-commerce for its graduate students. Vocational and technical colleges, high schools, and junior colleges are now involved too. You can find many levels of expertise right in your own backyard.

Don't try to go it alone. The Internet is too big and too confusing to be mastered by anybody in their spare time.

Fourth, review your marketing strategies and goals. Will e-commerce enhance them? Replace them? Detract from them?

Fifth, allocate enough money to do it right. The Internet is a very hot medium. The customers, whether commercial or consumer, have very high expectations about Web sites, and won't tolerate a shoddy or confusing site no matter how much they might want your product.

Well begun is half done.

LATIN PROVERB

And now, some considerations for your actual Web site:

Sixth, don't try to design your own Web site. Designing an attractive, effective, flexible home page and linked pages is a creative art. You would be foolish to prepare your own ads without understanding the design and content and market expectations. You'd be even more foolish to do so on the Internet.

This doesn't mean that you should not be involved. You have to be deeply involved in the process of design since nobody knows your products and customers better than you.

Seventh, how much should a good Web site cost? We've seen wonderful sites that cost around $1,000. We've seen horrible sites that cost tens of thousands of dollars. Approach it the same way you'd approach choosing an advertising agency. In fact, start with the agency you currently use. They may have developed the expertise, or can steer you to it. Ask other business owners whose sites you like.

Remember that e-commerce requires a sizable investment. It's a way to make sure that the world doesn't pass you by.

Eighth, what will people do at your site? What will they be looking for? Some will seek entertainment. Some will be casual surfers with no interest in your product. Others will look for information, solutions to problems, new insight into a process. Some will be shopping—so you want to make sure that they can make a purchase easily.

Ninth, designing a Web page is no simple task. The content has to carefully chosen. Navigation from the home page to other pages has to be smooth and trans-

Early in 1998 CDNow Inc., a Pennsylvania company that sells music and music publications over the Internet, linked up with Shinseido Company, a large music distributor, to move the company into the mainstream of the Japanese market. The deal has allowed CDNow not only to offer domestic Japanese titles, but also to market itself locally with Japanese-language advertising, newsletters and Internet-based chat groups. The company has also added the ability to let Japanese customers pay with yen credit cards. (*The Wall Street Journal*, July 12, 1999, R-22)

A study by the Massachusetts Institute of Technology's Sloan School of Management reveals that shoppers on the Internet attach relatively low importance to finding the lowest price. The study found, for example, that prices at Amazon.com, which has more than 80 percent of the market for on-line books, were far from the lowest offered on the Web in 98 percent of the comparisons made. Prices at Books.com averaged $1.60 less than the same books at Amazon. Yet Books.com has only two percent of the market. The researchers suggest that the reasons why are branding, awareness, and trust. "Customers don't really know if they're going to get the products, so they go with a company they can trust," researcher Michael Smith explains. (*The Wall Street Journal*, July 12, 1999, R-8)

parent and fast. Registering a Web site involves a number of steps: Register your domain name with internic.com and get listed on the major and the most appropriate search engines. You have to decide which kind of secure transaction mechanism to use, and explore the interesting world of shopping carts. Visit www.nowtools.com to get started.

Tenth, finally, once you have a Web site and enter the world of e-commerce, try a "soft opening" to work out the kinks. Ask your friends and allies to visit the site and give you feedback before going public (the same as you'd do with a restaurant).

There will be kinks, snags, errors, and problems. That's OK; the Internet is a new medium for business.

Don't be put off by all the negative comments we have made about e-commerce. Take them as cautions, amicable warnings to make sure that your venture into e-commerce is profitable and fun.

And now, gentle reader, onwards!

As in the traditional retail world, customer service is the key to success. Merchants who don't listen to their consumers and respond to their needs will fail on the Internet just as they would in any other sales channel.

KEN SEIFF, FOUNDER AND CHIEF EXECUTIVE OF BLUEFLY.COM, A DESIGNER OUTLET STORE THAT OPERATES IN CYBERSPACE

15

How Do You Evaluate Your Marketing Efforts?

"If you can't measure it, you can't manage it" is trite but true. Keeping track of results is the only way to improve your marketing efforts. Your marketing results may be measured in sales (dollars or units), greater market share, increased store traffic, inquiries, reduced complaint rates, number of press releases published or __________ (fill in the blank). There are plenty of ways to evaluate your marketing efforts if you take the time to think through what results you anticipate before beginning to run an advertisement, submit a press release, or publicize a sale.

Think.
MOTTO POPULARIZED BY IBM'S THOMAS WATSON

The paradigm of marketing evaluation comes from direct mail. Experienced direct mailers can tell how well an offer is doing within three days of the initial mailing. The rates of response, paid response, telephone and e-mail, and other inquiries are closely monitored and measured against past performance to determine whether or not to continue the mailing.

This works because direct-mail marketers measure everything they can and keep very detailed records. The method begins with testing two or more packages on a small but statistically significant portion of a mailing

Milwaukee-based Midwest Express, named the best domestic airline by Zagat Airline Survey, has been profitable since its second year, 1985. Even during the disastrous early 1990s, when the airline industry collectively lost $13 billion, Midwest continued to make money. It knows what its market wants: business travelers enjoy its competitive fares and discounts, its first-class sized leather seats, and wonderful meals served on china with linen napkins. (*The Boston Globe*, July 9, 1999, C-1)

list until they establish a control, a response that they feel is acceptable. They then test for:

- *Quality of the mailing list.* How do the results stack up against other mailing lists? Which list generates the best response? The fewest nixies (undeliverable addresses)?
- *Offers.* Which offers draw the best response? The worst?
- *Packages.* Which package (consisting of envelope, offer, letter, response device) pulls best?
- *Timing.* Which day of the week or season of the year pulls best?

They even test such arcana as "hand addressed" versus mailing labels, postage stamp (slightly askew!) versus imprint, envelope size, and color.

Make no mistake about it. This has become a very precise science. If a package meets their preestablished goals, they continue. They roll out the rest of the list—and test a new package against this control.

It takes patience. It takes cash. It takes fanatic attention to details—and it generates increasing sales over time. Is measurement important? You bet your shirt it is!

The test of a vocation is the love of the drudgery it involves.

LOGAN PEARSALL SMITH

You need clear goals against which to measure your marketing efforts. Goals have two components. They are time-bound, setting dates by which something is to be accomplished, and they require that accomplishment to be measurable. Otherwise, there is no way to determine whether or not you have reached the goal.

Although most goals will be expressed in dollars, many marketing goals have other measures:

- Improvement in market share
- Penetration of new markets
- Reduction in customer complaints
- Decrease in delivery times
- Increase in sales force and/or sales area
- Increased unit sales
- Change in size, timing, or content of orders
- Leveling seasonal sales fluctuations
- Increased hits on Web site
- E-commerce inquiries
- Number of requests for demonstrations, literature, information
- Positioning in the minds of a target market
- Top-of-mind awareness
- Percentage increases of revenue, profits, margins
- Mentions in media (favorable, one hopes)

Most dollar goals involve:

- Increase in revenue
- Increase in gross margin and profits
- Improved revenues in specific market areas

The Roosevelt Savings Bank used direct mail to announce the opening of a new branch. Most of their prospects lived within a five-minute drive, which made broadcast advertising too broad in scope. Their mailings used whimsical images and contained fun-filled offers. At the end of the six-week promotion, 377 new account relationships had been established, generating $5.8 million in new deposits. Within two months, the relationships that were established grew to more than $8.6 million in deposits. (*Direct Mail by the Numbers*, U.S. Postal Service)

There's no dearth of measurable marketing goals. The discipline to do this measurement is another matter, and totally in your hands.

The end may justify the means as long as there is something that justifies the end.

LEON TROTSKY

Keeping good records is a necessary element in evaluating marketing efforts. Your records provide the baseline against which you can measure progress or lack of progress.

Most businesses are seasonal to some degree. Sure, summer is a slow time for many businesses—but for others, it's the busy season. You have to know your seasonality if you are to correctly interpret your marketing results.

Restaurant owners learn quickly how the day of the week and the month of the year affect their sales. They have to juggle kitchen and wait-staff to cover the busy times, yet cannot afford to staff up during slow periods. Their staff wants to know when they will be busy so they can plan their own schedules.

Retail merchants have daily and seasonal fluctuations, too. Their hours (a marketing effort) should reflect the needs of their patrons. Many will have longer hours during the holiday season and will measure results against prior holiday seasons as part of their management effort.

Your accounting information has to be accurate if you are to measure margins and profits. If you don't measure margins and profits, perhaps you should work for someone else who does; you cannot make sane marketing decisions while ignoring these vital measures.

You must control your inventory to avoid stockouts during busy periods. How do you know stock levels are needed? Your records.

Daily, weekly, monthly, and annual sales by item, product line, specific service, target market, or segment should be part of your records. Again, this is baseline information.

Marshall Field, founder of Chicago's landmark department store, said that he knew that 50¢ of each advertising dollar was wasted—but he didn't know which 50¢ it was. This uncertainty about advertising can be a major frustration since the results of an advertising campaign aren't apparent for weeks, and in that time other factors may affect success of the campaign.

In order to evaluate your advertising, you have to set clear goals as part of the advertisement creation process. A good question to ask your ad agency is "How can we measure this ad?" If the agent shrugs and says he or she has no idea, go elsewhere—a well-designed ad, almost by definition, can be evaluated.

This begins with the purpose of the ad. Are you trying to generate additional sales? How much? More "top-of-mind awareness"? Surveys before and after can measure this precisely. Introduce a new product? Track inquiries before and after. More foot traffic? Sample the traffic and ask why they decided to enter your store.

When Patricia Gallup and David Hall founded PC Connection in 1982, mail order was their marketing strategy in order to get personal computers and information about them to consumers. By 1998, telephone, catalogue and Internet orders were generating $732 million in sales for PC Connection, and the company has won *PC World* magazine's World Class Award for eight consecutive years in the best online-mail-order catalogue category. (*The Concord Monitor,* July 1, 1999, A-1)

H.P. Hood, a Boston-based dairy, has a new pitch-person in their ads. The mission of Hood's "Answer Mom" is to create an ongoing dialogue with consumers about health, nutrition and Hood products. Since many consumers regard dairy products as the ultimate commodity, Answer Mom's job is to convince consumers about the added benefits of such Hood features as light-blocking bottles. She can also answer nursing mothers' questions and other inquiries regarding health. Hood envisions Answer Mom as a long-running campaign. (*The Boston Globe*, May 28, 1999, C-3)

If you are not clear on what you want the ad to do for you, you can't measure its effectiveness. It's that simple.

Nothing is particularly hard if you divide it into small jobs.

HENRY FORD

Which promotions worked for you and which didn't helps you establish a track record to evaluate future promotional efforts. If you look carefully at a given promotion and ask why it didn't work as well as you had hoped, you may be able to glean more information than from a successful promotion. After all, if the promotion worked, why analyze it further? (Answer: to find out why it worked so you can repeat it another time.)

Do not try to evaluate a promotion in isolation from the prevailing external environment. When you did a SWOT earlier (see page 27), you looked carefully at external factors such as the state of the economy and what the competition was doing. These factors can warp the results of a promotion. If you are selling luxury goods and plan a major sales push in December, what happens when the economy falls off the cliff in November? Your promotion "didn't work?" Or were stronger forces involved?

Success or failure may be due to economic conditions since people's purchasing behavior is a function of the economy. The stock market run-up of 1998 and 1999 biased the sales of luxury items (multimillion-dollar homes, expensive imported automobiles, climate-controlled wine cellars and humidors), which in ordinary times would be slow sellers.

Make sure you are measuring in context, in the big picture, not just paying attention to blips due to unusual conditions.

The door to success is always marked "Push."
American Proverb

Ask experts for help in evaluating your marketing efforts.

Ask your competitors. Few small business owners are able to answer this coherently, indicating the severity of the problem, and will welcome the chance to trade ideas.

Your trade association will address evaluation issues in their publications and in their trade shows. Everyone wants to improve their marketing—and the trade association wants to aid its membership.

Ask a Small Business Development Center for help. They are free, professional, and have access to a wealth of information. The Small Business Administration has free and low-cost marketing help. They both put on seminars addressing evaluation issues.

Ask a marketing professor for help. This kind of marketing problem is exciting for students as well as for owners, and is one of the least intrusive consultations since much of it can be done through secondary sources.

Consider hiring a marketing consultant to work through evaluating methods with you. This can be a one-shot deal or an ongoing relationship that will pay

The appetite for Big Macs and fries shows no sign of diminishing. In June 1999, McDonald's reached a milestone no other business in the world has ever achieved: the opening of its 25,000th store. It took 44 years for McDonald's to grow from Ray Kroc's first restaurant in Des Plaines, Illinois. About half its restaurants are outside the U.S., in 115 countries. More than 1,000 are located in Canada. (*The Wall Street Journal*, May 13, 1999, B-13)

for itself in saved marketing dollars and decreased opportunity costs.

Nobody has all the answers. But you can find most of them.

Coupons provide a good measure of whom a promotion reaches. They are often used to measure the efficacy of particular ads, and clearly are effective to judge from the ever-increasing size of the Sunday paper. Coupons are used to promote staples, commodities with very little differentiation such as canned soups, dry cereals, soaps, and butter substitutes.

What do you look for when you use coupons to measure marketing results?

- The rate at which the coupons are redeemed
- The number of coupons redeemed
- The percentage of coupons redeemed
- Increased sales of couponed items
- A feel for the elasticity of the target market
- The number of new customers

You have plenty of couponing options:

- Newspaper and magazine blow-ins, inserts, and cards
- Coupon decks for both consumer markets and special markets, such as small business owners
- Flyers
- Phone book coupons
- Accepting competitors' coupons

Many merchants use coupons as a prospecting tool, figuring that everyone loves a bargain and that once the coupon holder samples the merchant's wares they'll become repeat customers.

I can resist everything except temptation.
OSCAR WILDE

Special offers (sales, grand openings, discounts, new product introductions, and so forth) can be measured by increases in foot traffic as well as the more usual revenue and unit sale measures.

If your records do not include traffic (number of prospects entering your place of business), you will have a harder time measuring the effectiveness of your special offer. This is an important piece of information to maintain.

One of Andy's early clients kept records of weather conditions as well as foot traffic in his resort town art gallery. He argued that if he didn't, he couldn't separate out the bored weather-bound tourist count from the serious prospects, and thus couldn't determine the pull of a given artist or group of artists.

One of the most interesting aspects of e-commerce is that it comes with built-in measures of effectiveness: automatically recording the number of hits on a Web site, and offering the potential of gathering information on who visits.

Dick's Supermarkets, an eight-store chain in Wisconsin, uses transaction data from its loyalty-card program to personalize shopping lists that it mails every two weeks to nearly 30,000 members. Generated by Relationship Marketing Group's DataVantage software, the lists contain timed offers based on past purchases. A consumer who bought Tide several weeks ago, for example, may be offered a 50-cent coupon to restock. (*American Demographics*, March 1999, page 43)

Since it implemented eShare's NetAgent human-interaction software, 1-800-Flowers in Westbury, New York, has seen sales go up. This is good news, since 12 percent of its annual sales, or more than $40 million, is generated through its Web site. eShare's technology, which cost about $50,000, also reduced the load of customer e-mail queries by about 20 percent. A study by Jupiter Communications shows that cybershoppers seem to prefer live customer service for more complex transactions, like buying airline tickets and applying for loans. Converting browsers to buyers is a key reason many e-commerce sites add human interaction to their service strategy. (*American Demographics*, February 1999, page 37)

Make sure your Web site lets you know:

- How many visit your site
- How many stay and look at more than the first page
- How many register, sign up, or otherwise give you information on who they are
- How many make purchases at the site
- How many follow up with inquiries (e-mail, for example)

E-commerce is in its infancy but already has shown its power as an information and evaluation tool.

Benjamin Franklin may have discovered electricity but it was the man who invented the meter who made the money.

EARL WILSON

Glossary

Advertising: Paid commercial messages (in any medium) designed to inform, persuade, or remind potential or actual customers about a product or service.

After-sale actions: Those actions you take to retain a customer by providing additional benefits after the sale has been completed.

AIDA: An acronym for a sales "rule." Gain the prospect's "Attention," arouse their "Interest," pique their "Desire," and move them to take "Action."

Banners: Internet advertising you run on carefully selected sites where you expect to find your prospects and customers. The ads usually look like a banner (hence the name) and call attention to your own Web site.

Behavioral segmentation: A market segmentation technique based on different behaviors exhibited by consumers.

Benefits: What people buy, the "what's in it for me" that all consumers seek, as distinguished from features, the characteristics of a product or service that deliver benefits.

Branding: The techniques used to establish a brand name for a commodity. Successful branding examples: Coca-Cola, Kleenex, Xerox, Perdue Chicken. Currently used mainly in e-commerce for companies such as eBay (for auctions), Amazon (for books), iVillage (for a women's electronic community).

Browser: Software (such as Netscape) that is used to examine various Internet resources.

Cash cow: A Boston Consulting Group term for a business segment or product that provides cash flow and profits with minimal or no additional investment.

Category buster: A "big box" store or sales venue that contains an overwhelming amount of product choice and price for a single category such as toys (Toys Я Us) or hardware (Home Depot, Lowe's).

Clipping service: A service business that clips items and references from periodicals and other sources (increasingly from the Internet) according to parameters set by the client.

Collateral material: Promotional material in addition to paid advertising, which includes brochures, flyers, business cards, stationery, and other image pieces.

Commodity product: A product that is generic, such as hard red wheat or #6 bunker oil. These undifferentiated products are usually sold on price, since the perceived benefits are so similar between one barrel of oil and another, or between bushels of hard red wheat.

Competitive edge: Your competitive advantages over your most direct competitors.

Consumer demand: The aggregate demand for a given product or service in a defined market area. This is an important measure to determine for your product or service.

Core competency: What your business does best; its most important and central activity.

Cost structure: The analysis of all the cost factors in the production or marketing of a product or service, including burden or share of overhead.

Customer needs: Primary needs (physiological, safety, and security) and secondary needs (such as self-expression or status) have a big impact on buyer behavior. You should ascertain what customer needs your goods or services satisfy.

Database marketing: Compiling detailed consumer information in a database format allows marketers to precisely allocate marketing efforts to the most productive market segments for a given product or family of products.

Deliverable: The tangibles that you actually give to the customer, such as a consultant's bound report.

Demographics: The study of the characteristics of a population, such as age, gender, religious affiliation, income.

DINKs: An acronym for "Double Income, No Kids."

Direct mail: A marketing technique in which sales are generated by sending a direct mail package (advertisement, product offer, response device) to a mailing list.

Direct marketing: Marketing that goes directly to the prospect, either by mail, e-mail, catalog, telemarketing, or similar device. A wider term than direct mail.

Direct response marketing: A variant of direct marketing in which the prospect qualifies him or herself by responding to an offer. The offer may be presented as a coupon, a direct mail package, an 800 number in a space advertisement, or other means. By responding, the prospect indicates an interest in the offer.

Distribution: The physical movement of products and the establishment of intermediaries to facilitate this movement.

E-commerce: Short for "electronic commerce," and includes I-commerce as well as other forms of electronic commerce.

E-engineering: A new variant of re-engineering in which the business is reconfigured to take maximum advantage of the many e-commerce possibilities opening up.

Early adopters: The first group to purchase new and/or unfamiliar products or services, according to the Stanford VALS (Value and Lifestyle Study).

Elasticity: If a market is sensitive to price changes, buying less if the price rises or more if it falls, that market is said to be elastic. An inelastic market is relatively unaffected by small price changes.

Ethnic marketing: Marketing promotions aimed at a specific ethnic group, such as Hispanics or Asians.

Facility brochure: A brochure that explains the full range of services or products a firm provides its customers.

Focus groups: A market research technique in which a small number of people are brought together and interviewed, under controlled conditions, about their perceptions of the value of a product or service.

Full-cost pricing: Pricing that includes the fully loaded cost (product or service cost plus overhead allocation) of the product or service as part of the pricing formula.

Geographic segmentation: Market segmentation based on a geographic area. A convenience store might have a geographical market of a few blocks, while a supermarket chain may cover several states.

Home page: The main Web page, or Web site, for an individual, organization, or business.

I-commerce: Internet-based commerce, a narrower term than e-commerce though less commonly used.

Image: The managed perception of the general public of a person, business, or institution. This is an essential piece of the marketing mix.

Internet: The collection of interconnected computer based networks that all use a common protocol (TCP/IP) to share data.

Links: On the Internet, a method of connecting ("linking") one Web page with other Web pages, whether in the same or other networks.

Mail order: A request for goods or services that is received, and often filled, through the mail.

Market gaps: Areas in your market where there are untapped opportunities for you to take advantage of.

Market niche: A smaller fragment of a larger market that's especially suited to your unique abilities and your business's product or service.

Market research: Market research is the study of the demands or needs of consumers in relation to particular goods or services.

Market segmentation: A method of organizing and categorizing people or organizations who buy your products or services.

Market share: A portion, usually expressed as a percentage, of a market that a business operates in.

Marketing strategy: Action steps that delineate how your company will reach its marketing goals.

Marketing: All the activities involved in moving products and services from the producer to the consumer, including advertising, sales, packaging, promotion, and pricing.

Mass market: A large, undifferentiated, unsegmented market.

Meta tags: Words that appear in the header of a Web site's home page.

Multi-level marketing: A method of distributing goods and services that incorporates network marketing, direct selling, and person-to-person marketing.

Networking: A promotional tool for expanding your group of contacts, as well as building relationships in your field and in others.

Packaging: How your product is presented to prospective buyers.

Positioning: How you differentiate your products or services from those of your competitors and determine what market niche to fill.

Price ceiling and price floor: The "right" price for your goods and services will float somewhere between a "price ceiling" (what the traffic will bear) and a "price floor" (high enough to cover your cost and profit needs).

Product features: The characteristics or physical descriptions of a product, as opposed to "benefits," or what problems a product helps a customer solve.

Product life cycle: One of a product's four stages: introduction, growth, maturity, and decline. Each stage has certain characteristics that have a powerful influence on marketing.

Profit: The return on a business undertaking received after all operating expenses are paid.

Promotion: How you make your market aware of your product or service. Promotion includes advertising, public relations, special events, newsletters, networking, and public speaking.

Prospecting: A process of selecting likely customers from a group.

Psychographics: A method of segmenting a market that looks at a group's behavior patterns, attitudes, and expectations.

Public relations: Methods and activities that promote a favorable relationship with the public.

Qualify: Establishing certain characteristics that prospective customers must meet.

SINKs: An acronym for "Single Income, No Kids."

SITCOMs: An acronym for "Single Income, Two Children, Outrageous Mortgage."

Sociocultural segmentation: A method of segmenting a market that takes into account a group's religion, national origin, race, social class, and marital status.

SWOT analysis: A method of analyzing a business that looks at its "Strengths, Weaknesses, Opportunities, and Threats." This helps a business decide what to emphasize and what not to emphasize, and takes into account both internal and external forces.

Target market: Those people or organizations in your market who are most likely to buy from you.

Telemarketing: A sales tool that's also called telephone marketing.

Trends: The inclination of a market to favor a particular product or product feature.

URL: An acronym for *Uniform Resource Locator,* which is an Internet address.

VALS (Value and Lifestyle Structure): A study by Stanford Research Institute in the early 1980s that segments the buying public into nine categories according to values and lifestyles.

Web site: See *Home page.*

WOOPies: An acronym for "Well-Off Older People."

Index

E

F

G

H

I

T